Love Rescue Me

The Healing Power of Love

John O'Brien O.F.M.

Publisher: John, o.f.m.

Acknowledgements:

I would like to thank Michael Quilty for typing the manuscript and his helpful suggestions.
Also I would like to thank Jacqueline Corkish who helped with the art work and Stephanie Pastoris who helped put the whole thing together.

I would like to dedicate the book to all whose kindness helped me heal – the list is too long and the danger is I would leave someone out.

CONTENTS

Foreword 1st Edition 7

Foreword 2nd Edition 8

Introduction 9

Chapter 1   Beauty Will Save The World 11

Chapter 2   Love Is His Name 24

Chapter 3   I am My Beloved's and He is Mine 39

Chapter 4   The Look of Love 56

Chapter 5   The Dark Night of Love 69

Chapter 6   Dare We Hope 81

Chapter 7   Love, A Flame of Yahweh Himself 99

FOREWORD 1st Edition

Andy Ripley was a sporting legend in his time in rugby union, athletics and rowing. He then became successful in banking and business. However, in the last few years he had a pulmonary embolism and advanced prostate cancer.

As a child, he had been one of my sporting heroes and I met him in London at a rugby – writers function. I gave him a gift of my book "Rachel's Tears and Mary's Song". I was able to give something back to someone who gave me so much. He read the book when he was undergoing cancer treatment. He has now made a full recovery.

I wrote "Love Rescue Me" to help anyone in any kind of illness, from cancer to mental illness. Andy has become involved, in his new lease of life, in helping children's charities and health issues for men. Here are some of the musings he has given me on the new book (at the one time funny but with a hidden seriousness).

"Like a cast off from the father Ted show, there was Father John sitting besides me and we had a chat and we've been chatting ever since.

Father John has a way with words and a kindness and can smell desperate and struggle.

Now if you try to read this book sequentially from the beginning to the end, unless you have the intellect of a small Bavarian village you will by about page 55 find yourself struggling and desperate.

It is written in a meditative style and is meant to be read slowly and absorbed. It cannot be taken in one gulp. It can be read taking a section at a time, or sometimes even just a sentence or a word. Then one can think and play with that piece in one's mind and begin to feel loved, to feel healed, to feel OK with oneself.

It is a book to randomly dip into and find a word or a sentence that means something to you, just you and then think about and play with that word or sentence and it'll all be O.K.

How am I now today? Well I'm just fine. How is father John today? Well I reckon he's just fine too. The question we both want to know is, How are you?"

INTRODUCTION

People ask me what's the best way to read this work or indeed any of my work. What I have written is a form of shared prayer and reflection. It is written in a meditative style where the reader can pause, reflect and then move on and see the mystery explored from a slightly different angle. This was a type of writing I found in reading Irish literature where the readers found themselves part of the story.

I was inspired in this work by the artist Marc Chagall. He had hoped to renovate a little church on his estate in France. He planned to fill one room with his paintings based on the Song of Songs and when he entered this space he hoped to experience being surrounded by love and where there is love there is God. He didn't fully realize his scheme but donated his paintings to a museum in Nice. What he did with paintings I hope to achieve with word-pictures, poetry and sometimes poetry in prose.

The anchor for the word-pictures is the Song of Songs, or Canticle of Canticles as it is variously called. It's the love-poetry of the Bible. It is tempting to say it is secular as distinct from sacred, but in the eyes of God all is sacred especially love. I reflect initially on the text of the Canticle, which is a celebration of love, and then I reflect meditatively on the themes and ideas that it brings up for me. I share with the reader the reflections of those who helped me in their writings. When I was depressed their world of beauty helped me and led to a gradual healing. The readers may enter prayerfully into that place and allow themselves be immersed in the word-images of love. This does not exclude those who do not wish to enter the text in that way – I have no wish to exclude them from the love shared in the words.

My little apostles of love are Thérèse of Lisieux, Marthe Robin, Dante, Maurice Zundel, Charles Péguy, Etty Hillesum and Fyodor Dostoevsky. These are all people who loved deeply and their legacy in their writings has healed many and helped them discover their dignity. They have played an important part in my life. I use this motley crew to reflect on love. Where there is love there is God. The figure of Mary is a gentle presence in the book. There is a form of icon in the Eastern Orthodox churches called *Hodegetria* (from the Greek, 'female guide'). In it Mary never points to herself but she points to her son – every time I tried to write of Mary I found I was pointed to her son, to speak of him.

So I hope you, the reader, can share these reflections with me. I allow the reader find his or her own space in what I call my little 'gallery of love'.

Chapter 1

Beauty Will Save The World

"True Beauty is God and all that is gracious and good in the world is a manifestation of his Beauty" (Al-Kasiani, d.1330)

I remember a time when I was mired in depression and darkness. My journey to finding health took many twists and turns. On my journey different people living and dead helped me in one way or another. When I share the insights and love others gave me I am indirectly telling my own story.

Visions of beauty helped me in my dark days and remain with me on my journey. One of the artists who inspired me with his vision of love and beauty was the artist Marc Chagall (1887-1985). Beauty will save the world was the cry of Dostoevsky's *Prince Myshkin*. Marc and his friend Paul Klee were very interested in studying the art of the icon. This gave them their feel for otherworldliness and colour and harmony. Paul Klee described his friend's work as "tears that rise joyfully to heaven". Marc also spoke of the influence of the Bible:

> I went back to the great universal book, the Bible. Since my childhood, it has filled me with vision about the fate of the world and inspired me in my work.... I see the events of life and works of art through the wisdom of the Bible. A truly great work is penetrated by its spirit and harmony.... Since in my inner life the spirit and world of the Bible occupy a large place, I have tried to express it.

As a Jewish artist, Chagall did not address issues of sin and predestination. Chagall's Biblical message, one of the first conjunctions of modern art with the text, was one of human understanding, tolerance, and love.

Marc was a Russian born Jewish artist. He created his own vivid style reflecting Russian village life and Yiddish folklore. Later on in his life he spoke of his love for the person of Jesus. Chagall said that belief in Jesus can move the mountains of despair.

> "What counts is art, painting, a kind of painting that is quite different from what everyone makes is out to be. But what kind? Will God or someone else give me the strength to breathe the breath of prayer and mourning into my paintings, the breath of prayer for redemption and resurrection?"
>
> (Marc Chagall in *My Life*)

Chagall did know tragedy in his life. He saw the tragedy of his people in the Holocaust. One of his most famous paintings was the so-called white crucifixion which showed a Jewish Jesus martyred among his brothers and sisters under Nazi oppression. When he left France to live in the United States his wife Bella tragically died. Yet he never acceded to despair always praying for redemption and resurrection. Marc had a deep and sincere love for the Bible. He often remarked that he loved to read it, for he found it the "greatest source of poetry". He saw himself as an artist-poet using colour and image to lift the heart. Picasso was a master of the intellect, Chagall a master of the heart. He would also say that he did not just read the Bible but it allowed him to dream.

After the war Marc returned to France and re-married. On his estate in Vence, he found a disused church. There he had the idea of finishing his little church with paintings of biblical themes. They would form an ambience for prayer, like the icons he so much admired. One of his dreams was to decorate the sacristy with themes from the *Canticle of Canticles*. There he hoped to find himself surrounded by love and a celebration of life. In this his soul would find healing. He never fully realized his vision but he did embark on a series of paintings on the *Song of Songs* which he donated to the Marc Chagall gallery in Nice. Where there is love, there is God was Chagall's theme in the paintings. In one of the paintings are different themes from the Canticle. In it David is like a bird, and an old man plays the *'shofar'* of the feast – there is music, poetry, love and the Bible.

Chagall's dreams and visions helped me. The beauty of his work and the uplifting of the heart I experienced in looking at his work brought peace to me at different times. His vision of surrounding oneself with love and there realizing God is present is the guiding theme in this book of meditations on the *Song of Songs*, the *Canticle of Canticles*. My vision is to surround the reader with word-pictures of love and thereby healing. 'Beauty will save the world'

Love is as Strong as Death (Sg 8:6)

Pope Benedict XVI has called his first encyclical letter *'God is Love' ('Deus Caritas Est')*. In it he speaks about the Canticle and love. It is a beautiful description of what the Canticle is and how it relates to our life of faith. It is worth meditating on:

> Concretely, what does this path of ascent and purification entail? How might love be experienced so that it can fully realize its human and divine promise? Here we can find a first, important indication in the *Song of Songs*, an Old Testament book well known to the mystics. According to the interpretation generally held today, the poems contained in this book were originally love-songs, perhaps intended for a Jewish wedding feast and meant to exalt conjugal love. In this context it is highly instructive to note that in the course of the book two different Hebrew words are used to indicate 'love'. First there is the word *dodim*, a plural form suggesting a love that is still insecure, indeterminate and searching. This comes to be replaced by the word *ahaba*, which the Greek version of the Old Testament translates with the similar-sounding *agape*, which, as we have seen, becomes the typical expression for the biblical notion of love. By contrast with an indeterminate, 'searching' love, this word expresses the experience of a love which involves a real discovery of the other, moving beyond the selfish character that prevailed earlier. Love now becomes concern and care for the other. No longer is it self-seeking, a sinking in the intoxication of happiness; instead it seeks the good of the beloved: it becomes renunciation and it is ready, and even willing, for sacrifice.

He goes on to say that Jesus shows us the path of love which leads through the cross to the resurrection: the grain of wheat falls to the ground and dies and in this way bears much fruit (*Jn 12:28*). "Starting from the depths of his own sacrifice and of the love that reaches fulfillment therein, he also portrays in these words the essence of love and indeed of human life itself." *(Deus Caritas Est, no.6)*

His predecessor, Pope John Paul II preached on the *Song of Songs*. He said the "truth of love proclaimed in the *Canticle of Canticles* cannot be separated from the language of the body" (*L'Osservatore Romano*, 12 June 1984). In this he re-echoes the philosopher Simone Weil who said that to reproach mystics with loving God by using words of sensual love is as though one were to reproach a painter with making pictures by means of material substance. In the same catechesis John Paul gave on the Canticle he speaks of uniting physical and spiritual love in one.

Pope John Paul also hoped to make a contribution to healing the age-old rift between Christians and Jews. One cannot forget the prophetic image of his placing an apology for sins against the Jewish people at the Wailing Wall in Jerusalem in the year 2000. What is less known is his commissioning of the Pontifical Biblical Commission to teach in his name about the influence of the Hebrew Scriptures on our sacred texts. This document appeared in 2001 and over the years its influence will inform preachers, and teachers and hopefully create a new era of dialogue. The emphasis on the body through which we received information is seen in the prologue of the *First Letter of Saint John*:

> Something which has existed
>   since the beginning,
> which we have heard,
> which we have seen with our own eyes,
> which we have watched
> and touched with our own hands,
> the Word of life –
> this is our theme.
> That life was made visible;
> we saw it and are giving our testimony,
> declaring to you the eternal life,

> which was present to the Father
> and which had been revealed to us.
> We are declaring to you
> what we have seen and heard,
> so that you too may share our life.
> Our life is shared with the Father
> and with his Son Jesus Christ.
> We are writing this to you
> > so that our joy may be complete.
>
> *(1 Jn 1:1-4)*

The recurrence of such words as "see", "hear", "touch", "hands" shows the importance of the physical through which is meditated the divine and in this case the Word who is life. He has "seen" Jesus and "contemplated" his reality.

Every part of the Bible presupposes a believing community whose faith is sustained and affirmed by that part. Thus works like the Canticle were repeated, handed down, standardized (i.e. canonized) by the communal wisdom of generations. The poems that comprise the book probably (as we saw with Pope Benedict) began life as love poetry, maybe designed for a wedding celebration. It came to be read by devout Jews at the feast of Passover. This feast celebrated the great events of the Exodus where the people were saved from slavery and restored to health. The central part of the feast consists of firstly a recording of the Exodus, then a ritual meal followed by a reading from the Canticle. The reading of the *Song of Songs* in the context of the Passover is a demonstration that the event of salvation, in which God's people are established in the way of God's love, is workable in the setting of intimacy and love between people. This life is meant to be lived "now".

While the Canticle speaks of human love, it has become deeply beloved of mystics in the Christian and Judaic worlds. Rilke spoke of poetry opening up horizons that the poet might never have intended primarily. It is the same with the art of someone like Chagall. His pictures are poetry in paint and they speak to people in ways that the artist could never have imagined. It is not a case of either the "literal sense" or the more "spiritual, allegorical sense." It is a case of both-and. In one of the texts of the ancient rabbis, the *'Zohar Teruma' (143-144a)* it is said that "God returned to earth on the day the Canticle was given to Israel." Where there is love, there is God.

A. Choraqui, in his commentary on the Canticle wrote:

> "The association of ideas, the resonance of the words show the three levels at which it is possible – and necessary – to read the Canticle:
>
> - a canticle to the glory of pure love
> - a canticle celebrating the wedding of the soul dedicated absolutely to the Love which is God
> - an allegory which describes the eschatological fulfillment of the history of Israel."
>
> *(Le Cantique des Cantiques, p.58)*

These ideas are Choraqui's, a Jewish exegete of the Canticle, but they show us how the Canticle blooms and blossoms in the hands of the one who contemplates it.

Opening Prayer

St. Thérèse of Lisieux wrote the following words to her friend Pere Roulland *(LT226)*:

"This is, my brother, what I think of God's justice: my way is all confidence and love. I do not understand souls who fear a Friend so tender. At times when I am reading certain treatises in which perfection is shown through a thousand obstacles, surrounded by a crown of illusions, my poor little mind quickly tires; I close the learned book that is breaking my head and drying up my heart, and I take up Holy Scripture. Then all seems luminous to me; a single word uncovers for my soul infinite horizons, perfection seems simple to me, I see it as sufficient to recognize one's nothingness and to abandon oneself as a child into God's arms."

This part of her letter is one of the most beautiful she ever penned. I believe the true theologian is the one who prays. This is a saying that is closer to the Orthodox Church than to the Latin Church. Thérèse spoke of finding a Friend so tender and loving as our God is. I find the prayers of Jesus, Mary, and Joseph are a great source of prayer and abandonment into the arms of this Friend Thérèse spoke of.

Ps 103 is the psalm I have chosen to meditate upon. Friedrich Nietzsche once said that if we were more aware of what this psalm said we would abandon the position of seeing the Old Testament God and the God of Jesus as being opposed. There is one God and he is Love. Rabbi Abraham Heschel said that the caricature of the Old Testament God as vengeful while the New Testament God is one of mercy is the result of Christian anti-Semitism. We see in these standards why John Paul II asked the Biblical commission to inform the faithful about the Jewish people and the scriptures.

St. Thérèse's words form a structure in which we can understand *Ps 103*. The psalm begins with the following words:

> Bless the Lord, O my soul,
>   and all that is within me,
>   bless his holy name.
> Bless the Lord, O my soul,
>   and do not forget all his benefits –
> who forgives all your iniquity,
>   who heals all your diseases,
> who redeems your life from the Pit,
>   who crowns you with steadfast love and
>   mercy,
> who satisfies you with good as long as you
>   live
>   so that your youth is renewed like the
>   eagle's.

The call to blessing is turned towards the personal 'I' of the pray-er, it is turned towards his or her own innermost being. In John Paul II's catechesis on the Song of Songs in 1984 he said that the language of love between the person and the inner self opens another way to understand the Canticle. Georges Bernanos spoke of the fact that many people do not like themselves. Here the psalmist addresses his or her innermost being and points beyond the pray-er to the one who is the source of love and light. He is the one who loved us first *(1 Jn 4:10-16)*.

The psalmist goes on to acknowledge what God has done for him. He is the one who redeems, the one who delivers the person from everything that is life threatening. He is the one who "crowns you". The picture is that of a royal bridegroom prepared for the wedding (see *Canticle 3:11*). He crowns the beloved with steadfast love, that love that never fails and compassion which will be spelled out more fully in *v.13* of the psalm. He is the one who satisfies the soul's desire. John Donne (d.1631) compared the dawning of love as the spring scene which brings new life. He says:

Love's Growth

I scarce believer my love to be so pure
    As I had thought it was,
    Because it doth endure
Vicissitude, and season, as the grass;
Methinks I lied all winter, when I swore
My love was infinite, if spring make' it more.

But if this medicine, love, which cures all sorrow
With more, not only be no quintessence,
But mixed of all stuffs paining soul or sense,
And of the sun his working vigor borrow,
Love's not so pure, and abstract, as they use
To say, which have no mistress but their muse,
But as all else, being elemented too,
    Love sometimes would contemplate, sometimes do.

Verses 6-18 now turn to the parallel experience in the history of the people of God. This is a story which hinges on a God who works vindication or righteousness, a God who puts right what is wrong (see *Ps 7:9-11*), a God who guarantees justice for those on the receiving end of oppression. The events of *Exodus 33* are recalled. There Moses is seen as disconsolate and weighed down by the burden of leadership of a people who, in his temporary absence, had made a golden calf image, now turns to God and says, "Show me your ways, so that I may know you and find favour in your sight" (*Exodus 33:13*). The subsequent revelation to Moses leads to the classic statement of God's character in *Exodus 34:6*: "He God, the Lord, a God merciful and gracious, slow to anger and abounding in steadfast love and faithfulness..." This is the key to the understanding of God in *vvs. 6-18*. What God did in the past he does now in the present for the one who prays:

> The Lord works vindication
>   and justice for all who are oppressed.
> He made known his ways to Moses,
>   his acts to the people of Israel.
> The Lord is merciful and gracious,
>   slow to anger and abounding in steadfast love.
> He will not always accuse,
>   nor will he keep his anger forever.
> He does not deal with us according to our sins,
>   nor repay us according to our iniquities.
> For as the heavens are high above the earth,
>   so great is his steadfast love toward those
>   who fear him;
> as far as the east is from the west,
>   so far he removes our transgressions from us.
> As a father has compassion for his children
>   so the Lord has compassion for those
>   who fear him.
> For he knows how we were made;
>   he remembers that we are dust.
>
> As for mortals, their days are like grass;
>   they flourish like a flower of the field;

> for the wind passes over it, and it is gone,
> > and its place knows it no more.
> But the steadfast love of the Lord is from
> > Everlasting to everlasting
> > on those who fear him,
> > and his righteousness to children's children,
> to those who keep his covenant
> > and remember to do his commandments.

Theses verses celebrate the kindness and forgiveness of God. Charles De Foucauld once said that the one who has true compassion on us is the one who knows of what we are made. The *Letter to the Hebrews* celebrate Jesus; the high-priest who knows our weakness because he shared fully in the human condition and now intercedes on high for all his brothers and sisters.

The psalmist also speaks of God's kindness. The root of the Hebrew word for compassion is *raham*. This refers to one's innermost being. It describes the love of a mother for the child in her womb. Pope John Paul II explored the meaning of *raham* in his letter *Dives In Misericordia*. It is an image used by Isaiah to speak of God's love for his people and every individual:

> Can a woman forget her baby at the breast,
> Feel no pity for the child she has borne?
> Even if these were to forget you,
> I shall not forget you.
> Look I have engraved you
> on the palms of my hands
> > *(Is 49:14-16)*

Jesus' parable on the prodigal son in *Lk 15:11-32*, shows us the fullness of God's pardon and mercy. He gives his love to the one who hurt him.

Paul Claudel in one of his writings speaks of God as the Father with his children who has no need to be told of what we are made. He speaks of Mary, the mother of Jesus, as the sacrament of the maternal tenderness of God. Maurice Zundel, a Swiss priest who died in 1975 speaks of his conversion as a young man. He prayed before a statue of Mary and had an inner experience of the love in her heart. He, too, spoke of her as the sacrament of the maternal tenderness of God.

The figure of Mary has always been important in my life. At one stage in my life I was the victim of an assault. It was also at this time that I experienced bullying in college and elsewhere. My life was shattered and my physical and mental health deteriorated. One day when I was totally ill I felt the sensation of slipping away and seeing a great light. I was quite prepared to give in – not so bad this!

However at this time in Assisi there were two friends of mine – Susannah and Anita. They did not know I was ill but when they were at Mass in the Basilica of San Francesco they each said they saw my face in the host. After Mass one would not speak to the other about this vision. One was afraid of what the other might say – things like that weren't supposed to happen. Eventually they spoke and decided something must be wrong. They prayed before the Blessed Sacrament for hours, getting nowhere. Eventually, exasperated (a common experience in prayer) they asked God what he wanted. They heard an interior voice asking what had they to offer in prayer. They replied only all the love that was in their heart. They knew when they offered all that love their prayer was heard. It was at that moment I experienced a physical cure and came back. Later when I met them again Susannah told me "Our Lady" would always be a special person for me and would be a link of love for me.

The emotional cure is taking far longer than the physical cure, but as the years go on and I experience more and more healing I am able to bring some of the love I experienced to others. When I met the girls in 1980 there was no way I could have foreseen any of this. Needless to say there were many dark days in-between and in the face of depression, much confusion, but like St. Thérèse I return again to God's word and begin to pray again. *Ps 103* is one of my favourite prayers. The psalm finishes with the refrain:

> The Lord has established his throne in the Heavens,
> and his kingdom rules over all.

> Bless the Lord, O you his angels,
>> you mighty ones who do his biddings,
>> obedient to his spoken word.
> Bless the Lord, all his hosts,
>> his ministers that do his will.
> Bless the Lord, all his works,
>> in all places of his dominion.
> Bless the Lord, O my soul.

The psalm ends with a closing hymn to the one who "rules over all" *(v.19)*. All are summoned to bless him – angels (see *Ps 34:7,* cf *91:11*), all the mighty ones, all the hosts and ministers. When we bring our experience of God's grace with us to worship, we come in the company of all that exists in heaven and earth. In *Rev 5:13* we hear the following words: "To the one seated on the throne, and to the Lamb be blessing and honour and glory and might forever and ever."

Bob Dylan wrote a beautiful love song once. He called it "Love Minus Zero" (no limits). The name of the album was *"Subterranean Homesick Blues"* on this side of the Atlantic. In the U.S. it was called *"Bringing It All Back Home"* which is a title the producers thought might not go down so well on this side of the Atlantic. He began the song with the words:

> My love she speaks like silence
> Without ideals or violence
> She doesn't have to say she's faithful
> Yet she's true like ice, like fire.

Dylan provides the listener with a series of contrasts – the contrast between "without ideals" and "without violence" – both of which form that silence, and the contrast between the sometimes socially dulled faithful and true, and the qualifying, regenerative "like ice, like fire". In one of the legends of the early Fathers there is the story of the young man who asked the abba what more he must do. The abba told him, "Become fire!" The image Dylan uses of the one who speaks like silence describes for me the moments I abandon myself in prayer into the arms of the one St. Thérèse called 'Friend' and a most tender one.

The image of abandoning oneself into the arms of this friend is something that is found in *Ps 131*:

> O Lord, my heart is not lifted up,
>   my eyes are not raised too high;
> I do not occupy myself with things
>   Too great and too marvelous for me.
> But I have calmed and quieted my soul,
>   like a weaned child with its mother;
>   my soul is like the weaned child that is
>   with me.
>
> O Israel, hope in the Lord
>   from this time on and forevermore.

Cardinal Mercier one said that if we begin to realize God's great love then we are close to sanctity. St. John of the Cross spoke in his writings of sleeping in the arms of love and there being satisfied. Simone Weil once said that: "God and humanity are like two lovers who have forgotten the place of appointment. Both arrive at the fixed time, but at different places, but they wait and wait." It is in the silence of the heart that we find the place and time of the appointment.

Chapter 2

Love Is His Name

The Song of Songs, which is Solomon's.

The Bride	Let him kiss me with the kisses of his mouth.
	Your love is more delightful than wine;
	delicate is the fragrance of your perfume,
	your name is an oil poured out,
	and that is why the maidens love you.
	Draw me in your footsteps, let us run.
	The King has brought me into his rooms;
	you will be our joy and our gladness.
	We shall praise your love above wine;
	how right it is to love you.

(Song of Songs 1:1-4)

In his diary, Cesare Pavese, an Italian writer speaks of the problem of loneliness and it is only in his faith that he found the ultimate friend who does not deceive, that is God. He finds prayer the outlet to God, as if one is with a clear friend. He says: "All the problems of life are this: how does one overcome loneliness, how does one communicate with others." The couple in the Song of Songs find the cure for their loneliness in deep love. Pope John Paul in his discourse tells us that the first verses of the poem bring us immediately into the atmosphere of the whole Song in which the bride and bridegroom move in a circle irradiated by love.

The Hebrew title (*shir hasshirim*) usually translates as the 'Song of Songs' or the 'Canticle of Canticles'. This identifies the work as being superlative and a possible translation would be the 'Most Excellent of Songs" or perhaps the 'Most Sublime of Songs'. According to tradition King Solomon uttered some three thousand "proverbs" and a thousand and five songs in his lifetime (*1 Kings 4:32*). So by a fiction common at the time later wisdom works like the 'Canticle' were ascribed to Solomon.

The opening verses of the 'Song of Songs' are spoken by a woman. The Bible is full of stories in which male sexual aggression is often seen and assimilated into some of the most notable moments in redemption history (see Weems, *Battered Love*). The opening of the Song is a departure from this and shows us something new in the woman's craving for her beloved. Paul Claudel too points out: "The Song of Songs begins with a kiss" (Claudel, *Paul Claudel interogge*). "Such is indeed the start of the symphony" as Choraqui puts it. Saint Bernard says it is a pleasant discourse that begins with a kiss (*Sermons, p.87*).

In the Mediterranean area there is a tradition in which wine is a symbol of love. There is the figure of Alceo of Mitilene, Sapho. There is the celebrated *Rubayiat* of Omar Khayyam, the celebrated Persian poet who died in 1126. He spoke of love and wine. In the Bible itself wine is a symbol of pleasure, of every joy of life (*Qo 2:3; Is 22:13; Ps 104:15*). The experience of coming to know God is spoken of as 'tasting joyfully' (*Ps 34:9*) and we see in this why the Jewish tradition has seen in the kiss and the wine of the Song the luminous sign of God among his people. In the Christian tradition, too, many writers see the Father as the one who is thus implored: Let him kiss me. For the initiative in loving is his and he is the origin, and Father of all. He is the principle of tenderness, the source of love. All excellent gifts come from him. The mouth is his only son. "The mouth of the bridegroom", says St. Gregory of Nyssa, "is the source from which springs the words of eternal life (*Jn 6:68*): if anyone is thirsty, let him come to me and drink! For this reason the thirsty soul wants to offer its mouth to the mouth from which life springs by saying, "Let him kiss me with the kisses of his mouth." (*PG, 44*).

The kiss is the Holy Spirit. The Spirit is seen as the kiss that the mouth of the beloved Son imprints forever on our hearts (*Rm 5:5*). The same kiss eternally uniting the Father and the Son is now uniting us to them, so that, as Jesus says, "the same love with which you loved me may be in them" (*Jn 17:26*). Some other Fathers such as Cyril of Jerusalem and Ambrose of Milan see in the reference to the kiss and the wine an allusion to the Eucharist. Karl Barth in his *Church Dogmatics* was not comfortable with the manner of looking at the Song. He preferred the more literal reading of the Canticle where the lovers were seen in a new

Paradise, but I prefer a "both-and" approach where the literal and poetic open up new horizons.

The poem continues with the image of perfume and oil poured out. In Hebrew the word for name *"shem"*, sounds much the same as the word for perfume *"shemen"*. That's why the name of the beloved is like a perfume. She is telling him, your very presence is like a perfume.

The monologue finishes in verse 4 in which the woman cries out as if to say lead me into the marvelous adventure of love. The metaphor 'draw me after you' is used to express attraction, and the irresistible affect of the beloved. It is significant that Hosea uses the same verb. He is the prophet who spoke of love. He says of Yahweh: "I led them with reins of kindness, with leading strings of love" (*Ho 11:4*). The Hebrew word for "draw, lead" is *mashakh*. In Jeremiah we read: "Yahweh has appeared to him from afar. I have loved you with an everlasting love and that is why I draw you with kindness" (*Jr 31:3*).

The bride addresses her lover as king. There is a long tradition in love poetry, which can be traced as far back as ancient Egypt, where lovers address each other as king or queen, prince or princess. It can still be seen today - we hear of people dreaming of a prince charming. "Love is a kingdom where the poorest man is king". The king takes his bride into the private part of his house and his life. In the Bible the word used for the king's inner room is also the word used for the holy of Holies, the holiest part of the temple (*1Ch 28:11*). The word used for praising or extolling the king's love more than wine is *zkr*. This is the same word used in liturgical prayer in which we recall the good deeds of God and they become present to us when we pray.

In the first poem we read:

> He has taken me to the banquet hall
> and his banner over me is love.
>
> *(Sg 2:4)*

The banquet hall is a translation of the Hebrew word for wine-house and banqueting place. It is the house where love (wine) is to be celebrated. In *Cant 6:4* the bride is called a walled city. The banner represents the intent of the bridegroom not to take this city by storm but by love. As we saw at the start the bride is sick with love. St. Thérèse tells us "The malady of love is cured only by love". The bridegroom has reciprocated and his heart is full of love. He has no weapon but his very love. In the same way God does not conquer our heart except through an excess of love. The bride expresses her wound of love in the following way:

> Feed me with raisin cake,
> restore me with apples,
> for I am sick with love.
> *(Sg 2:5)*

The fragrances, images of the Song of Song have seemed strange to some to be used in our approach to God. Yet it is through the senses that we begin to grasp things and when the senses are purified we are brought closer to God. Father Donatien Mollat writes the following in his reflection on the writings of John:

> The word made himself visible, audible, tangible. It is through the senses that revelation came to men, that divine life was communicated to them, and it is in this way that they receive and welcome it. ... The use of sensory language to express the experience of communion with God in Christ is one of the characteristic features of Johannine spirituality. It is within the logic of the incarnation. *(DS, 8, c 217-224)*

This is a point that Origen, and after him all the great mystical tradition, has stressed very strongly: "Christ", he comments, "becomes the object of each sense of the soul. He calls himself the true light, to enlighten the eyes of the soul; the Word, to be heard; the bread of life, to be tasted; he is also called oil of anointing and nard because the soul is delighted by the perfume of the Logos. He became the Word made flesh, tangible, substantial, so that the inner man would be able to grasp the Word of life." (*In Canticum Canticorum, 142*)

Jesus, the Word made flesh, teaches us that God is love. He calls us "friends" and he shows us that one can have no greater love for one's friends than to lay down one's life for them (*see Jn 15:8-15*). He tells us that as the Father has loved him, so he loves us (*Jn 15:8*). In the first letter of St. John we read the following reflection on love:

> My dear people,
> let us love one another
> since love comes from God
> and everyone who loves is begotten by God and knows God.
> Anyone who fails to love can never have known God,
> because God is love.
> God's love for us was revealed
> when God sent into the world his only Son
> so that we could have life through him;
> this is the love I mean:
> not our love for God,
> but God's love for us when he sent his Son
> to be the sacrifice that takes our sins away.
> My dear people,
> since God has loved us so much,
> we too should love one another.
> No one has ever seen God;
> but as long as we love one another
> God will live in us
> and his love will be complete in us.
> We can know that we are living in him
> and he is living in us
> because he lets us share his Spirit.
>
> *(1 Jn 4:7-13)*

When we love we share God's spirit. His love has called us first and we find our home in him.

Being loved and aflame with love was something that touched the heart of St. Thérèse. She wrote:

One day, after Holy Communion, Jesus let me understand this sentence of the Song: 'Draw me; we run after the fragrance of your perfumes.' O Jesus, it is therefore not necessary to say: in drawing me, also draw the souls I love. This simple phrase, 'draw me', is enough. Yes, when a soul lets itself be captured by the intoxicating smell of your perfumes, it cannot run alone. All the souls it loves are drawn together with it; this is a natural consequence of its being drawn to you ... I feel that the greater the fire of love ignited in my heart, the more I will say, 'draw me', and the more the souls that will come close to me will swiftly run toward the fragrance of the beloved's perfume. Yes, they will run; we will run together ... for a soul that is afire with love cannot remain inactive."
(*Histoire d'une ame, 291-292, 295*)

St. Thérèse was an apostle of love and she helped a new generation to discover the inner core of love which is the heart of Jesus' message. It is to her that I now turn.

Love in the Heart of the Church:

Jesus tells us that his command for us is as follows: "Love on another as I have loved you" (*Jn 15:17*). This is how we reciprocate our friendship with him. St. Thérèse of Lisieux (d.1897) brought this message of love to a new generation. She lived Jesus' message in the confines of the Carmel of Lisieux, but her love radiated from there to the world.

When Thérèse was a child she was blissfully happy in a loving home, but then the lonely side of life manifested itself to her. On August 28th 1877 her beloved mother died. This was a great shock to the young and sensitive Thérèse. She was only four at the time. Her sister Pauline took over duties as mother. When Thérèse was nine Pauline decided to enter the Carmel at Lisieux. Thérèse spoke later of the anguish of her "little heart": "In a flash I beheld life as it really is, full of suffering and constant partings, and I shed most bitter tears." Thérèse developed severe headaches and fell chronically ill.

Her father asked for a novena of Masses to be said in the Paris sanctuary of Our Lady of Victories for Thérèse's cure. He also placed the family statue of Our Lady in Thérèse's room. During the novena, on Pentecost Sunday, May 13th 1883, the crisis reached its sharpest point. Tortured in mind and body Thérèse recognized nobody. Then Thérèse had the following experience which changed her life:

> Utterly exhausted, and finding no help on earth, I too sought my Heavenly Mother's aid, and entreated her with all my heart to have pity on me ... Suddenly the statue became animated and radiantly beautiful with a divine beauty that no words of mine can ever convey. The look upon Our Lady's face was unspeakably kind and sweet and compassionate; but what penetrated to the very depths of my soul was her gracious smile. Instantly all my pain vanished, my eyes filled, and two big tears rolled down my cheeks, tears of purest heavenly joy.
>
> 'Our Blessed Lady has come to me. She has smiled on me!' How happy I feel! But I shall tell no one, for if I do my happiness will leave me ... Then I looked down and recognized Marie. It was indeed to her and her earnest prayer I owed that wonderful grace, a smile from the Blessed Virgin! When Marie saw me gaze fixedly on the statue, she said to herself: 'Thérèse is cured'. It was true. The Little Flower had come back to life ... 'The dark winter was now passed, the rain was over and gone' and Our Lady's flower gathered such strength that five years later it unfolded its petals on the fertile Mount of Carmel.

Thérèse describes how she experienced that the statue seemed to disappear to be replaced by a vision of the Mother of God who was all tenderness and love and who smiled gently at Thérèse. She was cured and was strengthened to face life once more.

Later on in Carmel Thérèse would meditate on the figure of Mary. She said she longed to be a preacher so that Mary's life would be more appreciated. She was disappointed at some of the preaching she heard about Our Lady. "How strange that is! A mother who makes the glory of her children disappear! I think quite the opposite. I think she will increase the splendour of the elect … we know well that the Blessed Virgin is the Queen of Heaven and earth, but she is more mother than queen."

Mary's life at Nazareth is at the heart of what Thérèse would call the "little way" of love. Thérèse loved to contemplate Mary as the model of all Christians who live their love of God and neighbour in the ordinary circumstances of daily life. Jesus was fully human and the life he lived as a child was fully human too.

Thérèse wrote a poem in honour of Mary (*PN 54*). She speaks of Mary's life at Nazareth.

> No raptures, miracles, ecstasies
> Embellish your life,
> O Queen of the elect.

This refers to the hidden years of Jesus when he lived with Mary and Joseph. For Thérèse, Mary is truly the unsurpassable model of "little souls". She does not invoke her own story until the very last stanza:

> You who smiled on me
>   At the dawn of my life
> Come smile on me again…
> Mother… evening is nigh!

Thérèse had a picture of the icon of Our Lady of Perpetual Help which she kept in her breviary. She composed a poem in honour of the icon in 1897 and she asks for the grace to be strengthened in her ordeal.

> When I struggle, dearest Mother,
> You strengthen my heart in battle.
> Always, always, image of my Mother,

> Yes, you will be my happiness, my treasure,
> And I would like, at my last hour,
> To fix my gaze on you again.
>
> *(PN 49)*

Thérèse's Little Way:

When Thérèse entered Carmel she felt the call of many vocations. She would have loved to have been a priest, a prophet, or a doctor. She asked for martyrdom. Then she describes how she opened chapters 12 and 13 of St. Paul's first letter to the Corinthians. This is where St. Paul speaks of the charisms that build up the Church, but then he speaks of a better way:

> Set your mind on the higher gifts. And now I am going to put before you the best way of all.
>
> Though I command languages both human and angelic – if I speak without love, I am no more than a gong booming or a cymbal clashing. And though I have the power of prophecy, to penetrate all mysteries and knowledge, and though I have all the faith necessary to move mountains – if I am without love, I am nothing. Though I should give away to the poor all that I possess, and even give up my body to be burned – if I am without love, it will do me no good whatever.
>
> Love is always patient and kind; love is never jealous; love is not boastful or conceited, it is never rude and never seeks its own advantage, it does not take offence or store up grievances. Love does not rejoice at wrongdoing, but finds its joy in the truth. It is always ready to make allowances, to trust, to hope and to endure whatever comes.
>
> *(1 Co 12:31, 13:1-7)*

St. Thérèse says:

> "Yet strive after the better gifts, and I point out to you a yet more excellent way" (*1 Co 12:31*). And the Apostle

explains how all *the most PERFECT gifts* are nothing without LOVE. That *Charity is the EXCELLENT WAY* that leads most surely to God.

I finally had rest. Considering the mystical body of the Church, I had not recognized myself in any of the members described by St. Paul, or rather I desired to see myself in them *all*. *Charity* gave me the key to my *vocation*. I understood that if the Church had a body composed of different members, the most necessary and most noble of all could not be lacking in it, and so I understood that the Church had a Heart and that this Heart was BURNING WITH LOVE. *I understood it was love alone* that made the Church members act, and that if *Love* ever became extinct, apostles would not preach the Gospel and martyrs would not shed their blood. I understood that LOVE COMPRISED ALL VOCATIONS, THAT LOVE WAS EVERYTHING, THAT IT EMBRACED ALL TIMES AND PLACES.... IN A WORD, THAT IT WAS ESSENTIAL!

Then, in the excess of my delirious joy, I cried out: O Jesus, my Love.... My *vocation*, at last I have found it.... MY VOCATION IS LOVE!

Yes, I have found my place in the Church and it is You, O my God, who have given me this place; in the heart of the Church, my Mother, I shall be Love. Thus I shall be everything, and thus my dream will be realized.
(The Story of a Soul, p.195)

The heart of the Church is the place par excellence of the Holy Spirit in the Church. The heart is burning with love because it always contains the fire of Pentecost. The Heart that burns with love is first of all the Heart of Jesus and then all those united in love and Spirit with him.

In the last 18 months of Thérèse's life she lived her "little way" to the fullness. Her bodily health failed but she also experienced loneliness, doubt and the feeling of the loss of God. She describes her agony thus:

> Your child, however, O Lord, has understood Your divine light, and she begs pardon for her brothers. She is resigned to eat the bread of sorrow as long as you desire it; she does not wish to rise up from this table filled with bitterness at which poor sinners are eating until the day set by You. Can she not say in her name and in the name of her brothers, "Have pity on us, O Lord, for we are poor sinners!". Oh! Lord, send us away justified. May all those who were not enlightened by the bright flame of faith one day see it shine. O Jesus! If it is needful that the table soiled by them be purified by a soul who loves You, then I desire to eat this bread of trial at this table until it pleases You to bring me into Your bright Kingdom. The only grace I ask of You is that I never offend You!
>
> *(The Story of a Soul, p.212)*

And there is a darker passage later:

> Then suddenly the fog that surrounds me becomes more dense; it penetrates my soul and envelops it in such a way that it is impossible to discover within it the sweet image of my Fatherland; everything has disappeared! When I want to rest my heart fatigued by the darkness that surrounds it by the memory of the luminous country after which I aspire, my torment redoubles; it seems to be that the darkness, borrowing the voice of sinners, says mockingly to me: "You are dreaming about the light, about a fatherland embalmed in the sweetest perfumes; you are dreaming about the eternal possession of the Creator of all these marvels; you believe that one day you will walk out of this fog that surrounds you! Advance, advance; rejoice in death which will give you not what you hope for but a night still more profound, the night of nothingness."
>
> Dear Mother, the image I wanted to give you of the darkness that obscures my soul is as imperfect as a sketch is to the model; however, I don't want to write

any longer about it; I fear I might blaspheme; I fear even
that I have already said too much.
(The Story of a Soul, p.213)

Her last months were spent in deep loneliness and anguish. She lived intensely the suffering servant mysticism. The suffering servant is the one of whom Isaiah spoke "without comeliness, despised by all... yet by his wounds we are healed" *(see Is 52:13-53:12)*. The ones who share the suffering servant of Jesus are those who do not experience the Cross in great apostolic undertakings, but the ones who manifest God's hand in life's apparent absurdities: natural failings, physical defects, sickness, old-age and mental agony. The suffering servant is the one who allows God determine alone who and what one is. Thérèse experienced Jesus' sense of abandonment in Gethsemane and on the Cross. She shared Mary's grief at the foot of the Cross. Yet she also shared in their love and allowed God use this suffering to bring life to others – as did the suffering servant in Isaiah. Thérèse shared the anguish of her age and ours. She shared the loneliness of so many and it is in this sharing in a most radical, mystical way that Thérèse lived her vocation of love. She placed herself with the loneliest and most abandoned of souls that they might know they are not alone. She lived Jesus' command to love one another as he loved us in a radical way as a suffering servant.

St. Thérèse and her teacher, St. John of the Cross:

John of the Cross (d.1591) was a Spanish Carmelite who exercised a profound influence on Thérèse through his writings. Earlier we saw that there were not many authors that appealed to Thérèse – John was an exception. John wrote a version of the Canticle based on a contemplation of God as the bridegroom and the soul as the bride.

> Bridegroom
> She has entered in, the bride,
> To the long desired and pleasant garden,
> And at her ease she lies,

> Her neck reclined
> To rest upon the Loved One's gentle arms.
> (John of the Cross *The Spiritual Canticle* 28)

Thérèse wrote in her diary (p.103) describing how Jesus formed bonds in her heart that were stronger than blood. She quoted the following lines from St. John's Canticle:

> Following your footprints
> Maidens run lightly along the way.
> The touch of a spark,
> The special wine,
> Cause flowings in them from the balsam of God
> *(Canticle, 25)*

Thérèse describes how the first sermon she ever understood was a sermon on the passion. She also recalls one day while contemplating an image of Christ on the cross, she resolved "to remain in spirit at the foot of the Cross" (*MsA, p.99*). St. John of the Cross was the one for her whose words allowed her abandon herself "upon the waves of confidence and love" (*MsA, p.174*). Thérèse quotes these words of St. John in her abandoning herself to love:

> ... with no other light or guide
> than the one that burned in my heart.
> This guided me
> more surely than the light of noon
> to where he was waiting for me
> - him I know so well...
> (*MsA, p.105* quoting *Dark Night*, 4, 5)

John was for Thérèse the saint of love par excellence. St. Thérèse had great devotion to the Holy Face of Jesus which shared the true agony of the passion and the sense of abandonment and loss. On August 6th, 1896, Thérèse composed a 'Consecration to the Holy Face'. She introduces the text with two quotations from St. John:

> The smallest movement of pure Love is more useful to the Church than all other works put together.... Thus it is of the greatest importance that our souls be exercised much in *Love* so that becoming consumed quickly we do not linger long here on earth but soon attain to the vision of *Jesus, Face to Face.*
> *(LT 245)*

The first quotation is taken from the Spiritual Canticle B (stanza 29). Thérèse did not take the last phrase from the original. The second quotation comes from the *Living Flame of Love*, stanza 1, explanation of verse 6. Thérèse modified the translation a little. The original reads:

> It is, then, of the greatest importance that the soul exercise herself much in Love in order that, consuming herself rapidly, she hardly stops here below and arrives promptly in seeing her God Face to Face.
> *(GC II, p.1129)*

Here is another passage from John's *Living Flame of Love* that was precious to Thérèse. He wrote:

> This flame of love is the spirit of its Bridegroom, who is the Holy Spirit. The soul feels him within itself not only as a fire that has consumed and transformed it but as a fire that burns and flares within it, as I mentioned. (...) Such is the activity of the Holy Spirit in the soul transformed in love: the interior acts he produces shoot up flames for they are acts of enflamed love, in which the will of the soul united with that flame, made one with it, loves most sublimely.
> *(LF, 1 commenting on verse 3)*

Thérèse describes how Jesus looks for us and however far we may think we are from him he will transform us in flames of love (*LT 197*).

Paul Claudel who had a conversion experience on the same day as Thérèse (Dec 25th, 1886) wrote the following lyrical passage in honour of Thérèse:

> Your sacrifice is pleasing, Mademoiselle Martin! This pyre, completely united with its victim, which is your body and soul, God himself has swooped down upon as in the days of Elijah, to set fire to it. O, holy Virgin, it isn't the oil missing from the lamp of which the Canticle speaks – *lampades ignis atque flammarum* ["The flash of it is a flash of fire" (*Sg 8:6*)] – it is your Spouse Himself who is responsible for setting the fire! "I have come to bring fire to the earth" (yes, yes, to this same clay you inherited from Adam), "and how I wish it were blazing already!" [*Lk 12:49*] Burn, then, Thérèse! Burn, flame fed by your own breath! Burn black, burn clear, holocaust, until I have decomposed you in flesh and spirit! Burn, candle! What does she mean, this little girl burning like a Pentecost, asking me that My will be done, as if that must not be started by her; My will, as if it was not hers first to bring fire to Mine? As if, even the soul already all prepared, there remained no body through which complete consumption can take place? *Who will devour like I do?* says the fire.
> (Claudel, *Three Saints for Our Time*, p.82-83)

Chapter 3

I am My Beloved's and He is Mine

"Dodi li wa'ani lo"

The dream of loving and being loved is something we all cherish. The Canticle shows us that this hope can be fulfilled. It is as much a canticle of hope as of joy and love – indeed all three are intertwined. In the life of faith we see in some special lives that love and universal compassion are made real in their person. Gandhi loved the Beatitudes and practised them radically. In his Asherim he had a picture of Jesus placed in a prominent place. He said the love of one person is worth more than the hatred of a million. St. Seraphim of Sarov (1759-1833) was one of Russia's best-loved saints. He spent many years in seclusion before he opened his door to receive many visitors. He was famous for his love of children and his healings. His spiritual life was marked by the experience of light as witnessed by the disciples at Mount Tabor. Motovilov, one of Seraphim's friends, spoke of experiencing this light. We live in an age where we have come to doubt such phenomena. When Motovilov left Sarov to return to Moscow, he wondered about the reality of his experiences in Sarov. We have become used to domesticating transcendence and not trusting religious experience.

Indeed, Seraphim himself anticipated how difficult it would be for people to accept the stories as true, and he explained the cause of that skepticism: 'There is nothing incomprehensible here. The failure to understand comes about because we have wandered far from the spacious vision of the early Christians. Under the pretext of education we have reached such darkness of ignorance that now we find inconceivable what the ancients saw so clearly that even in ordinary conversation the notion of God's appearance did not seem strange to them. Men saw God and the grace of his Holy Spirit, not in sleep or in a dream, or in the excitement of a disordered imagination, but truly, in the light of day.'

Yet it is quite understandable that people should doubt the witness of other people to extraordinary happenings since with the passage of the years we human beings can even come to doubt the reality of extraordinary events in which we ourselves have taken part. Take, for example, what Elie Wiesel, the famous Holocaust survivor, said one day to a friend. Wiesel had been complaining that people have forgotten about the Holocaust and are behaving as though it was not a reality. To which his friend responded, 'Elie! Do you believe it happened?' Wiesel was taken aback by his friend's question and then slowly replied, 'No! I who was there – I do not believe it happened.'

Indeed Elie Wiesel was so overcome by the magnitude of the evil he experienced that he sometimes thought: 'Could it have actually happened?' Yet many of us are more prepared to accept the great manifestations of evil and become inured to the death of the innocent, especially children. When, however, people like Seraphim, and Marthe Robin show us an example of radical love rooted in God, it is then that we question. Even in the face of the tangible evidence many can believe in the presence of great evil rather than in the manifestation of love. This never discouraged St. Seraphim. He said that if one soul found peace then a thousand were saved, and that the aim of the Christian life was to receive the Holy Spirit.

Winter Past:

For this meditation, word-picture on love, I come to the following song:

> THE BRIDE I hear my Beloved.
> See how he comes
> leaping on the mountains,
> bounding over the hills.
> My Beloved is like a gazelle,
> like a young stag.
>
> See where he stands
> behind your wall.
> He looks in at the window,
> he peers through the lattice.

My Beloved lifts up his voice,
he says to me,
'Come then, my love,
my lovely one, come.
For see, winter is past,
the rains are over and gone.
The flowers appear on the earth.
The season of glad songs has come,
the cooing of the turtledove is heard
in our land.
The fig tree is forming its first figs
and the blossoming vines give out their fragrance.
Come then, my love,
my lovely one, come.
My dove, hiding in the clefts of the rock,
in the coverts of the cliff,
show me your face,
let me hear your voice;
for your voice is sweet
and your face is beautiful.'

Catch the foxes for us,
the little foxes
that make havoc of the vineyards,
for our vineyards are in flower.

My Beloved is mine and I am his.
He pastures his flock among the lilies.
Before the dawn-wind rises,
before the shadows flee,
return! Be, my Beloved,
like a gazelle,
a young stag,
on the mountains of the covenant.
(Sg 2:8-17)

In *v.8-9* the lover comes to his beloved before the dawn. This follows the time of waiting in the dark night of loneliness and expectancy. Now she knows winter is past and there is a new dawn, not just the dawn of a new day, but of a new spring. The presence of the lover is like springtime, love makes everything grow anew.

The lover has crossed over many mountains and fields "like a gazelle", like "a young stag". The passage from Isaiah where Yahweh comes to visit his people comes to mind:

> How beautiful on the mountains,
> are the feet of one who brings good news,
> who heralds peace, brings happiness,
> proclaims salvation,
> and tells Zion,
> 'Your God is king!'
>
> Listen! Your watchmen raise their voices,
> they shout for joy together,
> for they see Yahweh face to face,
> as he returns to Zion.
>
> Break into shouts of joy together,
> you ruins of Jerusalem;
> for Yahweh is consoling his people,
> redeeming Jerusalem.
> *(Is 52:7-10)*

The young lover now finds himself at the home of his beloved Shulamite. There he addresses her. The woman's voice is the one heard throughout. She describes to us the call of her lover. *Vvs.10-13* are a tender invitation to leave her home and come with him. There is an ancient Sumerian love song which parallels the call of the lover.

> My sister, why do you remain locked in your home?
> Little sister, why are you closed-in in your house?

We can be locked in by fear, hurt and disappointment. I know that place too. Yet if we remain patient love can still find a way through. The lover tells the beloved "winter is past, the rains are over and gone. The flowers appear on the earth". Then he goes on to describe how the whole horizon has been transformed in a musical chorus of souls and voices ("glad songs" and "the cooing of the turtledove"). He describes the blossoming fig tree, and the vines giving off their fragrances.

Psalm 65 celebrates new life in the spring in the following words:

> You visit the earth and water it,
>   you load it with riches;
> God's rivers brim with water
>   to provide their grain.
>
> This is how you provide it:
> by drenching its furrows, by leveling its ridges,
> by softening it with showers, by blessing the first-fruits.
> You crown the year with your bounty,
> abundance flows wherever you pass;
> the desert pastures overflow,
> the hillsides are wrapped in joy,
> the meadows are dressed in flocks,
> the valleys are clothed in wheat,
> what shouts of joy, what singing!
>
> *(Ps 65:9-14)*

The lover calls the beloved to take courage and come with him. "Come then, my love, my lovely one, come". It is an invitation to the total abandonment of love which opens up new horizons and a new creation. It is an invitation to leave her closed world. In leaving her old world she gives heart to all who are afraid of love, but in the end reach out. He tells her "your voice is sweet and your face beautiful". We find it hard to imagine God can say that of us, yet he says look at my son who gave his life for you - 'I love you' is his eminent message.

There is a worry about the little foxes that can wreak havoc in the vineyards. The lovers are real. They know the course of true love is never smooth, but they are going to take their courage in their hands and continue to deepen their love.

Then there is the beautiful declaration of the Shulamite woman. She tells her lover that she is his, that they are one: "I am my beloved's and he is mine" – "*dodi li wa'ani lo*". These words echo the words used in the book of Deuteronomy about the covenant made between God and his people: "…he will be your God…" and "…you will be his very own people" *(Dt 26:17-18)*. The lover is described as one who pastures his flock among the lilies. The use of the term "among the lilies" in Hebrew also conveys the desire of the lover for his beloved and now she tells him she is his, they are one. It conveys the idea of waiting and hoping for love. Rimbaud is once reported to have said: "*J'attends Dieu avec gourmondise*". I await God with "*gourmondise*". *Gourmondise* is not easy to translate. It conveys the idea of waiting for a meal with relish, looking forward to the laughter, love and the festivities. It conveys expectant, joyful, hope. Yet as much as we wish God to come to us, he also wishes that we come to love him too. Then both of us can say "I am my beloved's and he is mine".

Marthe – Surrender to Love:

Marthe Robin (1902-1981) was a French woman who lived out a life of profound union with God in the love of the Spirit and radiated that to others. She was born to Joseph and Amelia Robin in the region of the plateau (La Plaine) near Châteauneuf-de-Galaure. The year after Marthe's birth a typhoid epidemic struck and Marthe's sister Clemence (aged 5) died. The typhoid also affected Marthe's health. The young Marthe was a cheerful and happy child. At the age of 10 she made her first Holy Communion. She believed that Our Lord and herself became one at that moment. As a young girl Marthe enjoyed laughing, singing, dancing and telling funny stories.

Two years later, her health deteriorated and she began to endure severe headaches. One day in November 1918, she fell in the house and was unable to raise herself. Partially paralysed and stricken by a debilitating and mysterious illness (possibly some form of sleeping sickness or inflammation of the brain), she spent the following thirty months in a near comatose state, obviously in pain and suffering, crying out on occasions. She hardly moved or spoke, she ate practically nothing, and she dozed virtually all the time. It was thought that she would die and in April 1921, aged 19, she received the last rites of the Church. To everyone's astonishment, she rallied instantly and demanded to get up.

Marthe recovered her strength slowly and could walk only with the aid of sticks. She spent a great part of the next eight years quietly embroidering baby clothes, reading, and praying, sitting in an armchair in the kitchen. In the spring of 1922, she was looking after her sister Gabrielle's house nearby, while Gabrielle was absent in Marseilles. Poking around in the attic, Marthe opened an old trunk and found a book of religious reflections, "The Imitation of Christ". Two phrases in the book made an immediate impression on her: 'Your way will be one of suffering' and 'One must give God everything'. Shortly after this, Marthe's health worsened again. Her eyesight weakened and she could walk now only with great difficulty. It was arranged that she should go on the diocesan pilgrimage to Lourdes, but at the last minute Marthe gave up her place in favour of a sick person from a neighbouring village.

Marthe offered her suffering to Christ, and on 15 October 1925 when she was 23, she set down the first of her spiritual writings, many of which were dictated to various women friends and are regarded as family treasures by members of the Foyers.

In *'Consécration Totale à l'Amour et à la Volonté de Dieu'*, an act of complete abandonment to the will of God, she wrote at length about love and made herself a living sacrifice to God: 'O adorable Saviour! You are the unique possessor of my soul and of all my being! Receive the sacrifice that each day and at every moment I offer you in silence'. She dedicated her prayers and suffering to 'the good of the millions of hearts that do not love you, for the conversion of sinners, for the return of those who have gone astray and the infidels, for the holiness and apostolate of all your well-loved priests, and for all creatures'. From that time on, Marthe had one overwhelming objective in life: to offer herself entirely to God.

In October 1926, she became seriously ill once more and was again given the last sacraments. Marthe had long been a devotee of Thérèse

Martin, the saintly Carmelite nun of Lisieux who had died in 1897 at the age of 24 and whose 'little way' of simple, childlike and trusting Christianity had become so popular throughout France. Thérèse had been canonized in 1925 and now appeared to Marthe in three separate visions. The saint told Marthe that she was not going to die but that she would live and carry on Thérèse's mission, making it more universal.

About this time, Marthe said that 'suffering is the best school in which to learn true love' and she constantly offered her pain and her anguish to God. Eighteen months later, her legs became twisted and permanently paralysed. God was simply taking what she had already offered him. A local carpenter made a small divan and it was placed in a downstairs bedroom: on that divan Marthe was to spend the rest of her life.

Soon afterwards, she lost the use of her hands. She was now paralysed from head to foot, unable to eat and drink, and without even the solace of sleep. The most her parents could do for her was to wash her and occasionally moisten her lips with water or coffee.

Her soul was being formed in a special way. Later, Marthe was to insist greatly on the importance of silence. This is a necessary condition for listening to the Holy Spirit who speaks in the intimacy of the heart, "the divine silence of love". Marthe also received visions of Our Lady, and Mary was to play an important part in Marthe's life. She was like St. Seraphim in this way. He, too, received many visions of Mary. Once when Seraphim was ill Mary came to him with St. John (the Evangelist, or the 'Divine' as he is called in the East). Mary said to St. John "He is one of us" and Seraphim was cured and carried on his mission of love and healing. Again like Motovilov some question the reality of experiences of goodness and light which appear extraordinary – yet we have the witnesses who received the fruits of love from Seraphim and Marthe.

Marthe went through a long period of misunderstanding, ill health and disappointment between 1926 and 1928. Her illness and incapacity made her feel useless. She was tempted to disbelieve. Yet she turned again to Jesus and she wrote the following in her journal on 22nd

January 1930: "After many years of agony, of sinfulness, after all the physical and moral trials, I dared, I chose Jesus Christ". She would say later that the heart of Jesus was the place where she had chosen to live. The heart of Jesus is the heart of love aflame in the Holy Spirit. From then on Love was her life. She surrendered into his hands and abandoned herself to his loving purposes. Later that year she became a member of the Third Order of St. Francis. She was inspired by the love of the crucified. This took place during a parish retreat given by 2 Capuchin friars in December 1928.

One of the Capuchin friars who gave the parish retreat that year and introduced Marthe into the Third Order, Pere Marie-Bernard, told her that her vocation was to be like St. Francis, to be so united with Jesus that he lived in her heart. Marthe prayed over this and she began to see that this was true. She accepted the friar's words as an "infusion of the Holy Spirit". The Holy Spirit had taken hold of her and given her the strength to abandon herself to Jesus. She wrote later in her journal:

"The more and more my life is submitted to God and conformed to that of the redeemer, then the more will I be able to achieve his work. Thus, uniting my obscure work with the oblation of the infinite victim, uniting my unknown prayers for people, all my sacrifices, all my sufferings and all my immolations, and even the apparent uselessness of my life, I am sure this will not just be for my own sanctification, but I will be able to give to God an immense crown of the elect".

Like St. Seraphim had said when one soul found peace then a thousand are saved or as Gandhi said the love of one is worth more than the hatred of a million. Marthe found peace in her offering and later made her act of abandonment to God's purposes:

> My God, take my memory and all its recollections; take my heart and all its affections; take my understanding and all its faculties; make them serve only for your greater Glory. Take my entire will, and I will merge it in yours. No longer what I want, O most sweet Jesus, but always whatever You want. Take me... receive me... direct me. Be my guide. I abandon myself entirely to

You. I give myself to You a little host of Love, Praise
and Thanksgiving, for the Glory of your Holy Name, for
the enjoyment of your Love, for the triumph of your
Sacred Heart, and for the perfect accomplishment of all
your designs in me and around me.

More and more people heard about Marthe and they were drawn to her
for prayer and comfort – which they found. Marthe prayed that her
heart would be a place of love and welcome and that any troubled soul
that would come her way would receive peace, light and consolation.
She had tremendous devotion to the Sacred Heart of Jesus and she
prayed her heart and that of Jesus would become one in love. The heart
in the Bible stands for the emotive, sensitive part of the person and
Marthe wished that her heart would be as sensitive as the heart of
Christ. A little prayer she composed for Christmas shows her sensitivity:

> Divine Child Jesus, have pity on people who are all
> alone; have pity on lonely souls. Take care of them all
> and gather them to yourself on this evening's Feast, this
> night of Love, this dawn of peace and hope; so that their
> pain-filled hearts and troubled minds may find a refuge
> with their most loving, tender, all-powerful and true
> friend.
> If I can feel them huddled near You, O my King, all
> my sufferings will melt away, forgotten in love.
> Holy Child of the manger, who brings blessings and
> joy to the world, come into the souls who await You,
> who call to You, and make your heavenly dwelling
> within them, the house of your rest, your blessed manger.

Marthe continued to suffer. From 1936 onwards she shared mystically
in the death of Jesus. During the week she could not eat, drink or sleep
– she now spent all her time in prayer, but now her soul was full of love
and she suffered in love. She was like the suffering-servant spoken of
by the prophet Isaiah *(Is 52:13-53:12)*; the one who was disfigured yet
was the one who healed his people. Jesus was the supreme suffering-
servant and Marthe was united to him in a loving way, bringing his love
to a new age. In one of her visions of St. Thérèse she received the

message to carry on Thérèse's mission of love. Marthe would later remark humorously regarding this request from St. Thérèse: "Oh that hussey, she's left it to me".

In 1934, Marthe helped found a girls school. Later, with Fr. Finet, Marthe was to found the *Foyers de Charite* in 1936. In French, the word *foyer* literally means hearth. The hearth in a country house stands for the place where the family meet. The hearth is the actual heart of the family. Marthe hoped through this movement that many would experience in silent retreats the love and peace she had found. Over the years she met many of the retreatants. Another book could be written about these encounters alone. Marthe and Jesus had become one – " I am my beloved's and he is mine". Her gentle presence led and still leads many into that same intimacy. Mary is the one who consoled her and showed her the way to this union.

Sharing Marthe's Struggle:

Marthe could say that she lived in God, that Jesus himself lived in her (26 Dec 1929). Her vocation was to live in union with him, not in the way she had dreamt of but now as a suffering servant. She learnt that love was the core: "All for love, and all will be divine; to divinise all so that all will be sanctified; to love so as to expiate, to love so as to merit, to love so as to support, to love so as to console, to love so as to understand, to love so as to give, to love so as to forget oneself, to love so as to pardon, to love so as to love, to love so as to heal, to love so as to give new life" (5 Dec 1930). In her union with Jesus especially in his sufferings she learnt from him not to tremble, she learned absolute confidence in God. She was a missionary of love on the cross, "a chalice to contain love…", so as to pour this love on the world (5 Dec 1930). She knew her weaknesses and prayed all the time she be sustained by her beloved.

She spoke of Our Lady in the following terms:

> The most beautiful mission of Mary is to carry to Jesus all those who come to her … Let us follow Jesus and let us follow him with his incomparable mother, let us attach

our gaze not only on his humanity, but on his sacred humanity, on his suffering humanity: Jesus is the perfect model, the complete model, the model for all.

(3 Feb 1930)

Mary is beautiful with the very beauty of God. She is full of his Spirit. Saint Maximilian Kolbe said that the true Immaculate Conception was the Holy Spirit. Mary was uniquely united with God's Spirit. Sergii Bulgakov had a similar intuition in the Orthodox Church. Marthe, also, saw Mary as being uniquely united with the Holy Spirit. This special union is the basis for the doctrine of the Immaculate Conception, and made it possible for her to bring forth Christ. It also makes her a powerful intercessor for Jesus' brothers and sisters universally. Marthe's insights came to light when she met Pere Manteau-Bonamy in the 1940's.

Marthe experienced this "spiritual maternity" of Mary like the "beloved disciple" in St. John's gospel who took Mary to his home after Jesus, on the cross, had given her to him as a mother *(Jn 19:25-27)*. Mary was crucified in Spirit. The agony of Mary and Jesus continues in all who suffer and Marthe wished to be united with them in their universal love. She prayed that her heart would sing forever the pure Canticle of Love, and that she would follow her Lover (Jesus) step by step along the path of love, united with Mary. From 1930 onwards Marthe had another insight from the Holy Spirit. From this time on her only nourishment was the reception of the Eucharist once a week. Once after receiving the Eucharist she was given to understand that God was pointing her in a new direction, and giving her light into his merciful love for his Church, and how he had need of her to help reveal this love for his Church. She felt asked to give herself totally by love to his love, and to live her life in complete abandonment to the divine will of the Father. She began her work with the Foyer about this time, starting with a school for children. Like Jesus, and St. Seraphim, she loved children, and had a special place in her heart for them. She believed that God could not resist the prayers of the little ones.

She spoke now of being joyful, rediscovering happiness. Her unique communion with God made her a person of great joy. She spoke as if the "inner place of her heart" was a place where God enjoyed to play. When she felt his presence she felt she was in Paradise (19 Feb 1936). She wished all the world to experience this place of joy.

She called the Holy Spirit the consoler of our afflictions, the one who animates all our joys, the sacred source of every spiritual life. She prayed that our human nature be caught up into the divine unity. She prayed for a harvest of love (26 May 1939).

Marthe meditated on the following passage from St. John's gospel:

> On the last day, the great day of the festival,
> Jesus stood and cried out:
>
> 'Let anyone who is thirsty come to me!
> Let anyone who believes in me
>   come and drink!
>
> As scripture says, "From his heart shall flow streams of living water."
>   He was speaking of the Spirit which those who believed in him were to receive; for there was no Spirit as yet because Jesus had not yet been glorified.
>   *(Jn 7:37-39)*

She meditated on the cross of Jesus where blood and water flowed from his side *(Jn 19:34)*. He died to give us life in his Spirit. She composed the following prayer: "Lord, renew your first Pentecost ... Holy Spirit, Spirit of Love, come as a powerful wind ... Bring to the world the freshness of your sanctifying breath" (26 May 1939).

A Story:

There are many stories people have of meeting Marthe, and how her kindness, love and compassion brought healing to their troubled souls.

Many tell of how just a few words of kindness and love turned their lives around. For instance a philosopher went to see her in the 1950's. He was very serious and Marthe jokingly asked him if he had seen her goats. Marthe had a great sense of humour. He wondered why she asked him this. Later when he met her again he asked her why she spoke about goats. Her reply to him was that one should keep things simple in life and in thought. She helped him relax and they became great friends.

One of my favourite stories about Marthe's kindness concerns the former boxer Tim Guenard who is still alive today. When he was three his mother deserted him. At the age of five he was beaten severely by his father and spent three years in hospital with a broken body and broken heart. His placement in foster homes brought him little more than disillusionment and a growing sense of being deprived of love, and this would eventually lead him to harden his heart against love to keep from being hurt.

He found himself on the streets of Paris and struggled daily with hunger, cold and violence. Tim found himself lonely and broken. He tried to hide his loneliness and his broken heart behind a veneer of toughness, and this led him to lead a life of violence. Dante spoke in his *Inferno* of the centre of Hell as being frozen love. Tim had to wait till later in his life before love would break through and melt his frozen heart.

When he was 16 a judge gave him the chance to become a stone-engraver. It was the first real kindness he ever experienced and he honoured her trust. A policeman introduced him to the world of boxing. He didn't like policemen as such but he later remarked, "You never forget kindness, it gets written in your secret heart". This was the gift Marthe had and Tim was to meet her at a later point in his life.

A friend of Tim, Jean-Marie, told Tim stories about a pilgrimage to Chartres. The world Tim was used to meant that he couldn't imagine a pilgrimage with so many people together without someone coming to blows. Jean-Marie brought to his mind the l'Arche community. On one occasion a little boy who was handicapped put his hand on Tim's and said to him: "Tim you're nice". The boy's name was Philip. The love of a child allowed love enter Tim's heart again. It was the first day of a new creation. Tim met Father Thomas Philippe, co-founder of l'Arche, at Trosly-Brueil with Jean Vanier. Fr. Thomas Philippe loved Tim deeply and guided him gently. In boxing Tim had fought every boxer as if that boxer was his father but now he was learning that love was stronger than hate.

At l'Arche, when Tim worked there, he noticed a boy called Frederic struggling with a typewriter. Frederic had a broken body and could only type with difficulty. He was hurting his broken body trying to type. Tim was worried about Frederic and he tried to stop him hurting himself. On Tim's birthday Frederic pushed his wheelchair over and pushed a note into Tim's hands. It was Tim's 21st birthday and Frederic had spent the last month trying to type a birthday card for him. It was the first birthday present Tim ever received. He remembered the time he spent in hospital with no visitor, no presents. Frederic's kindness was now written forever in Tim's heart.

Tim fell in love with a woman called Martine, and Fr. Thomas Philippe advised them to do a retreat at Chateauneuf. The retreat was given by Fr. Marie-Dominique, Thomas's brother. They heard during the retreat that they had to meet the mystic, Marthe Robin. Tim felt unworthy, he still was developing confidence and was a little afraid. He tried to hide his fear by acting in a macho manner. As it happens he and Martine were the first called to see Marthe. I'll allow him tell the story:

> "But, we didn't even sign up!...
> The eyes of two hundred retreatants turn toward us. I turn beet red.
> I have no choice, I follow my wife. We make our way up to the Robin farm, up on a plateau. A rustic kitchen with a wood stove has been turned into a waiting room. People are speaking in whispers. A young girl leads Martine and me into a dark room. It seems very mysterious. We sit down near a bed barely discernable in the darkness. I imagine that this holy woman will immediately see into my soul and chase me away with a resounding "Out, Satan!" No, it's a clear, surprisingly

young voice emerging from the shadows to welcome us. We tell this invisible woman that we're newlyweds and very, very different from one another. She laughs!

She laughs and says:

"For the Good Lord, that's only an illusion. Your relationship must be based on Faith, Hope and Love."

Martine tells her we're expecting a child. She rejoices and marvels. She speaks of children as if she had raised them her entire life.

I tell her about my fears of becoming a father, considering my less-than-encouraging background, and about my dread of recreating the wounds I received. She listens then answers:

"Your children will grow to the measure of your love."

These words become inscribed within me with letters of fire.

As we're explaining our plans to move to Lourdes and to find a house, she stops us:

"A house to welcome those whom the Blessed Virgin will send you!"

Martine and I look at each other. Ever since our engagement, we've dreamt of a home we could share. Without knowing us, Marthe gives us confirmation and reassures us, saying:

"The Blessed Virgin will show you."

By the end of our meeting, in spite of the darkness, we can now make out this little body, curled up under a sheet, whose voice is as soft as an angel's and whose words are light.

Having made our way back out to the courtyard of this farm, we're blinded and astounded by what we have just experienced. This simple moment, of such importance in our existence, is a real cornerstone. Here we are, full of hope, thrilled. Marthe Robin would forever hold a place of utmost importance in our life.

(Stronger Than Hate, p.194f)

Tim was released by Marthe's words and heart of kindness. He knew the ravages of alcoholism and violence, and he didn't see how could someone like himself could change. But Marthe showed him love and told him that his children would grow to the measure of his and Martine's love. The first days of the creation of love begun by Jean-Marie, Philip, Frederic and Thomas-Philippe were now brought to fruition by Marthe's kindness. The love that was in Tim, but locked away, was now released.

Tim even came to forgive his father. Now he lives with Martine outside Lourdes and together with his family he looks after disturbed children. As Tim said, deep down we never forget kindness, it gets written in "our secret heart". This was one of Marthe's great gifts and her love gave birth to love in others.

Chapter 4

The Look of Love

Chapter 4 begins with a description of the beauty of the bride. This form of praise of the beauty of the beloved is called a *wasf* and is found in ancient Syrian scriptural songs. There are 4 wasfs in the Song of Songs (*4:1-7, 5:10-16, 6:4-10, 7:1-9*). Three of them describe the beauty of the woman.

> How beautiful you are, my love,
> how very beautiful!
> Your eyes are doves
> behind your veil.
> Your hair is like a flock of goats,
> moving down the slopes of Gilead.
> Your teeth are like a flock of shorn ewes
> that have come up from the washing,
> all of which bear twins,
> and not one among them is bereaved.
> Your lips are like a crimson thread,
> and your mouth is lovely.
> Your cheeks are like halves of a pomegranate
> behind your veil.
> Your neck is like the tower of David,
> built in courses;
> on it hang a thousand bucklers,
> all of them shields of warriors.
> Your two breasts are like two fawns,
> twins of a gazelle,
> that feed among the lilies.
> Until the day breathes
> and the shadows flee,
> I will hasten to the mountain of myrrh
> and the hill of frankincense.
> You are altogether beautiful, my love;
> there is no flaw in you.

> Come with me from Lebanon, my bride;
>> come with me from Lebanon.
> Depart from the peak of Amana,
>> from the peak of Senir and Hermon,
> from the dens of lions,
>> from the mountains of leopards.
>
> *(Sg 4:1-8)*

This is a form of eroticism that does not know vulgarity or abuse. It does not know malice or hypocrisy. It speaks of love and enjoyment and mutual sharing. He refers to her as the "mountain of myrrh and hill of frankincense". The Hebrew word for "frankincense" (*lebona*), which also appears in *3:6*, plays on the mountain name Lebanon. It's as if the lover says to his beloved, "I will fall wherever you like once it's into your arms". The poem speaks of the delight the couple take in each other.

The lover praises the eyes ... the hair of the beloved. Her hair is compared to a flock of goats moving down the slopes of Gilead. These may not be images that speak to the modern. Renita Weems, in her commentary on the Song of Songs, makes the following observation, which has always tickled my funny bone:

> Song of Songs is an ideal text for comparing the changing history and context of romantic talk. The poet uses the language and imagery of a rustic, semi-pastoral culture to evoke passion and desire. Comparisons to goats, gazelles, and apple trees sound strange to those of us who reside in parts of the country where neighbourhoods are treeless, apartment complexes have no lawns, and we ride underground in the earth's belly to get to our windowless downtown offices. We do not recognize seduction of the Song of Songs sort when we hear it. Our lives are too hurried and harried to bother with cryptograms from another time and another culture. And while it may be true that much of the speech in this little book is hopelessly lost on our modern ears because it does not speak to our experience, we must admit that

our own language for intimacy is equally lost on those unfamiliar with our culture. How does a generation flatter and woo one another when they are raised on microwave ovens, computers, fax machines, voice mail, the Internet, camcorders, electronic games, space fantasies, and overnight express mail? How do they talk about love? "You've pushed the right button," perhaps. Or "My hormones are in warp speed for you"? The maiden and her suitor of Song of Songs would stagger down the slopes of En-gedi in amazement and laughter at the sound of twenty-first-century erotic speech.

(Weems, NIB, V 395)

The lips utter delightful words. In the same vein the author of *Ps 45* whose "heart is stirred by a noble theme" writes that the bride whispers a continuous poem "to the king" (*Ps 45:2*). Her cheeks blush near the fire and appear like two halves of a cut pomegranate. If the apple is the fruit of the bridegroom, the pomegranate is that of his love (*4:3, 13; 6:7, 8:2*). These two love fruits express the reciprocity of the love between the bride and bridegroom.

The beauty of the bride has been attributed in the Christian community to the community of believers (*Ep 1:4; Col 1:22; Ph 2:5; Jude 24; Rv 14:5*), to Christ himself (*Heb 9:14, 1 P 1:19*) and to Mary:

> "Tota pulchra es, Maria,
> et macula originalis non est in te!"
>
> "You are all beautiful, O Mary,
> no stain is to be found in you."

O Garden of Paradise

Later on in the wasf the beloved is compared to a closed garden with many fragrances and spices. She is a place of beauty and delight. When John Paul commented on the 'closed garden' he compared it to the innermost, sacred part of ourselves which he addressed as feminine. The passage has also been used to speak of Mary. The English name 'Mary' comes from the original Hebrew name 'Miryiam'. The etymology of the name 'Miryiam' is unsure. Philippe Madre in his imaginative work on an icon of Our Lady, *L'icone de Marie-Porte du Ciel (p.33-39)*, suggests the following as a possible etymology of the name. He suggests firstly a composition of two words: *'mir'*, which means myrrh, and *'am'*, which means ocean, or maybe *'em'*, which means fountain. 'Mary' can mean an ocean or fountain of myrrh. Myrrh is a symbol of love. It's an attractive proposition and opens the way for us to meditate on the words of the love-poet of the Canticle:

> A garden locked is my sister, my bride,
>   a garden locked, a fountain sealed.
> Your channel is an orchard of pomegranates
>   with all choicest fruits,
>   henna with nard,
> nard and saffron, calamus and cinnamon,
>   with all trees of frankincense,
> myrrh and aloes,
>   with all chief spices –
> a garden fountain, a well of living water,
>   and flowing streams from Lebanon.
>   (Sg 4:12-15)

The garden image, like that of the vineyard in *2:15*, is used here of the beloved. It is an image that has continued from Egypt and Mesopotamia, to Greece and right down through the centuries. Tennyson once spoke of his love: "One rose of the rosebud of girls". The girl is a sealed garden or spring from which the lover longs to drink and find life.

The delights of the garden are then evoked. It is an orchard – the Hebrew here uses the Persian loan word *'pardes'* from which comes our word paradise (*Qo 2:5*). In it grow pomegranates and all kinds of delectable fruits. It is a garden that produces all kinds of perfumes and spices. This has featured already in the Song: nard, henna, myrrh (*1:12-13*), and frankincense *(3:6)*. Saffron mentioned here is a scented powder produced from the dried, crushed stigmas of the saffron crocus. Calamus or sweet cone is a type of wild grass that gives off a gingery smell. Cinnamon comes from the bark of a tree and was used as an ingredient in sacred, consecrating oil (*Ex 30:23*). An aloe was an aromatic resin derived from a tree native to India. All these fragrances and spices link in one-way or another to the attractiveness of the beloved. She is an "orchard" filled with "fruits and spices" evocative of love. The garden has in it a fountain (*v.15*), a fountain of clear, running water that comes from its source in the Lebanon hills.

Is the girl unattainable? No, the girl says in reply:

> Awake, O North wind,
>   and blow, O South wind!
> Blow upon my garden,
>   let its fragrances be wafted abroad.
> Let my beloved come to his garden,
>   and eat its choicest fruit.
>
> *(4:16)*

She summons the wind to carry fragrances from her garden to her lover. She invites him to enter the garden and taste its choicest fruits. Quickly he responds:

> I come to my garden, my sister, my bride.
> I gather my myrrh with my spice.
> I eat my honeycomb with my honey.
> I drink my wine with my milk.
> Eat, O friends, and drink:
> Drink deeply, O Lovers.
>
> *(5:1)*

He comes to share the fruits of her love. The last two lines of *5:1* are probably a comment by the daughters of Jerusalem encouraging the lovers to have their fill of the love that unites them. The daughters of Jerusalem form a type of chorus throughout the Canticle. The words are reminiscent of Ben Jonson's poem:

> Drink to me only with thine eyes,
>   And I will pledge with mine.
> Or leave a kiss within the cup,
>   And I'll not look for wine.
> The thirst that from the soul doth rise
>   Doth ask a drink divine;
> But might I of Jove's nectar sup,
>   I would not change for thine.

In the Christian tradition the 'closed garden' has had a Mariological interpretation. This is of course allegory – the original poem was a celebration of love and in the Christian tradition this came to be applied allegorically to Mary. The idea the poet had in mind was the idea of generation and new life, as shown by the fountain that irrigated the garden. The idea then is of a sacred garden or space. The closed garden speaks of a sacred space that is at the centre of the woman, and indeed as John Paul commented, is at the centre of us all.

M. Luker in his study of Biblical symbols speaks of how the closed garden became a garden of roses in medieval spirituality, and Mary the rose of roses. He speaks of the symbolism of myrrh, too, as a sign of Mary's participation in the death of her son at Golgotha.

Dante's Journey

The poet Dante Alighieri (1265-1321) can help us appreciate the Canticle in both its literal and its allegorical use by the mystics. He lived in troubled times, being exiled from his native Florence and suffering much in exile. He conceived his epic poem *The Divine Comedy (La Divina Commedia)* as a poem that brought us on a journey out of misery into the heart of love, which is God. When Dante was young he fell in love with Beatrice Portinari, who became his muse. Hans Urs Von Balthasar wrote of this love: "The love, which began on earth between two human beings, is not denied, is not bypassed in the journey to God; it is not, as was always, naturally enough, hitherto the case, sacrificed on the altar of the classical *VIA NEGATIVA*; so it is carried right up to the throne of God, however transformed and purified. This is utterly unprecedented in the history of Christian theology" (*Glory of the Lord*, vol III, p.32). There is the human need, the desire for the love that surpasses all others, which we only find with the heart of God. Then as Coventry Patmore says, re-echoing *Ps 131*, "the babe is at its mother's breast, the lover has returned to the beloved" (see *Underhill, Mysticism, p.135*).

Dante's journey takes him through Hell (*Inferno*), through to Purgatory (*Purgatorio*) then on to Paradise. This is his journey on the way to rest in God's love. Beatrice is his guide in the poem. Here in Paradise he hopes to find rest "as a child in its mother's arms, as the lover belongs to the beloved". In his *Convivio* Dante wrote that as the sun illumines all things and gives life by its warmth "so God vivifies all things by his goodness" (*Conv III, XII, 7-8*).

In Paradise Dante looked at the figure of God's love revealed in his son, Jesus.

> I see the cross as it flows forth with Christ,
> Yet cannot find the words that will describe it.
> *(Par XIV, 103-104)*

For Dante the one who follows Christ and takes up one's cross can understand what he was unable to put into words. The crushing defeats of his life – his exile, his distress at the tragedies and situation of the Church and Empire, all his sufferings and failures – are finally clarified and given ultimate meaning in the glorious victory of Christ on Calvary who overcame death. "Love is as strong as death" (*Sg 8:6*). As Dante nears his final homecoming to God the Father, Beatrice now tells him it's time for her to hand him over to other teachers. She points him to the vision ahead:

> Why are you so enamoured of my face
> that you do not turn to the lovely garden
> flowering in the radiance of Christ?

> There is the Rose in which the Word of God
> took on flesh, and there the lilies are
> whose fragrance led mankind down the good path.
> *(Par XXIII, 70-75)*

There Dante uses the imagery of the Canticle and the sealed garden. He points to Mary, the mother of Jesus, who brought the Word of God to us in the flesh. Dante's attention to Beatrice and then to Mary echoes the typical medieval piety that instinctively gravitated towards Mary and women saints because they mirrored the warm, maternal aspects of God's love.

St. Bernard, the contemplative "soul rapt in love's bliss", now assumes the role of Dante's guide. He is the one who will describe the beauty and order of the celestial rose. Bernard tells Dante to look at Mary:

> "Now look at that face which resembles Christ
> the most, for only in its radiance
> will you be made ready to look at Christ."
> I saw such bliss rain down upon her face,
> bestowed on it by all those sacred minds
> created to fly through those holy heights,
> that of all things I witnessed to this point
> nothing had held me more spellbound than this,
> nor shown a greater likeness unto God;
> and that love which had once before descended
> now sang, *Ave, Maria, gratia plena*,
> before her presence there with wings spread wide.
> *(Par XXXII, 85-93)*

Bernard then prepares Dante for the pilgrim's ultimate vision: to look at Christ. Before they can turn their eyes upon "the Primal Love," that is, God, they must pray for the grace to do so, since human power cannot attain to that, Bernard then addresses his famous prayer to Mary, which is the beginning of the final canto of *Paradise*:

> O Virgin Mother, daughter of your son,
> most humble, most exalted of all creatures

> chosen of God in His eternal plan,
> you are the one who ennobled human nature
> to the extent that He did not disdain,
> Who was its Maker, to make Himself man.
> Within your womb rekindled was the love
> that gave the warmth that did allow this flower
> to come to bloom within this timeless peace.
> For all up here you are the noonday torch
> of charity, and down on earth, for men,
> the living spring of their eternal hope.
> *(Par XXXIII, 1-12)*

He goes on to praise Mary as the one who ennobles our human nature, in whose womb the fire of love was relit and who is "… for us the torch of love's high noon". He echoes the words of the Canticle:

> The maidens saw her, and proclaimed her blessed,
> queens and concubines sang her praises
> *(Sg 6:9)*

Dante now enters into the divine vision of the Triune God, empowered by the divine grace given through the prayers of Mary, the love of Beatrice and the guidance of Bernard, he becomes overwhelmed by the "Light Supreme" of God's glory. He prays to God that his mind will be able to put this into verse so that "more of your might may be revealed to men". He then understands his vision as a divine gift for the salvation of the world. Like St. Paul, he perceives a revelation from God as a charismatic gift for the good of all. Dante said he had an experience of God's love in his heart and he hoped to communicate this in verse. He did not give details of his experience. He hoped he would lead the readers to their own experience.

Dante put these words on his vision as he entered into communion with the light:

> Within Its depthless clarity of substance
> I saw the Great Light shine into three circles
> in three clear colors bound in one same space;

the first seemed to reflect the next like rainbow
on rainbow, and the third was like a flame
equally breathed forth by the other two.
How my weak words fall short of my conception,
which is itself so far from what I saw
that "weak" is much too weak a word to use!
O Light Eternal fixed in Self alone,
known only to Yourself, and knowing Self,
You love and glow, knowing and being known!
That circling which, as I conceived it, shone
in You as Your own first reflected light
when I had looked deep into It for a while,
seemed in Itself and in Its own Self-color
to be depicted with man's very image.
My eyes were totally absorbed in It.
As the geometer who tries so hard
to square the circle, but cannot discover,
think as he may, the principle involved,
so did I strive with this new mystery:
I yearned to know how could our image fit
into that circle, how could it conform;
but my own wings could not take me so high –
then a great flash of understanding struck
my mind, and suddenly its wish was granted.
At this point power failed high fantasy
but, like a wheel in perfect balance turning,
I felt my will and my desire impelled
by the Love that moves the sun and the other stars.
(Par. XXXIII, 118-145)

Looking Unto Jesus (Heb 12:2)

Dante wrote:

> I am one who, when
> Love inspires me, takes careful note

> and that gives meaning to what
> he dictates within my heart.
>
> *(Purg XXIV, 52-54)*

Yet Dante was a man in his time who had come through the most bitter suffering: he had been publicly maligned, maltreated and despised. He endured physical hardships and moral bewilderment over his own sinfulness and over the corrupt and chaotic state of Empire and Church. He had been pushed to the very limits of endurance, to the edge of despair. He knew well the temptation to vengefulness, spite and revenge. Yet Dante had an experience of God's grace. The love he had for Beatrice had prepared him for this experience. He does not tell where or when his experience occurred but it overflowed into his work *The Divine Comedy* (*La Divina Commedia*). He came to see that one can love God and be loved in the midst of affliction. Umberto Cosmo says Dante was a "victim designated for the highest purposes of Providence, so that from the dust of misery he might reveal himself a prophet, apostle and soldier to a world back on its hinges. Misfortune was the price of glory which would come to him" (*L'Ultima Ascesa, p.189*). The experience of love for Beatrice was the spark that led him out of himself. He wrote his poetry "to remove those living in this life from the state of misery and lead them to a state of happiness."

The love of Beatrice led him to know the love of God revealed in Jesus. He was very influenced by the Franciscan tradition. He was influenced by Saint Bonaventure's picture of Francis of Assisi. For Bonaventure, Francis is the fulfillment of the soul's journey into God. To reach this end one must "seek the spouse, not the teacher, God not man, darkness not clarity, not light but the fire that totally inflames and carries us into God by ecstatic unctions and burning affections. This fire is God and his furnace is in Jerusalem and Christ enkindles it in the heat of His burning passion" (*Soul's Journey into God, 7:6*). These ideas helped shape Dante's verse. Bonaventure says of Francis:

> When the true love of Christ had transformed his
> lover into his image and the forty days were over that
> he had planned to spend in solitude and the feast of
> St. Michael the Archangel (Sept. 29) had also arrived,

> the angelic man, Francis, came 'down from the mountain' (Mt 8:1) bearing with him the image of the Crucified, which was depicted not on tablets of stone ... but engraved in the members of his body by the finger of the living God.
>
> *(The Life of Francis, 13, 1)*

"It is not by our own power that we are transformed but it is looking beyond ourselves into the face of love revealed in Jesus" (*Heb 12:2*). His love transformed Dante and he calls us to share in the love he experienced "to lift us out of misery".

Final Prayer

Just as St. Bernard of Clairvaux (1090-1153) was a guide for Dante so he can guide us when our feet weaken or we feel inadequate. In the Canticle we read:

> Set me like a seal on your heart,
> like a seal on your arm.
> *(8:6)*

St. Paul says of the Holy Spirit that he is the seal, the image of the bridegroom, which the Father engraves on the heart of the believer (cf *2 Co 1:22*, also *Ep 1:13* and *4:30*). Thérèse discovered this fire of love by looking at the face of love revealed in Jesus: "Adorable face of Jesus, only beauty that ravishes my heart, deign to imprint in me your divine resemblance, so that you may not look at my soul without looking at yourself" (*Histoire d'une Ame, p.258*).

Bernard in his time took up the same theme and shared his belief in God's merciful love. When we look to our own misery we can be overcome, but by looking unto Jesus we can receive the seal of love on our hearts. St. Bernard says in one of his homilies on the Song of Songs:

"I have shown to you that any soul, even laden with sins, captive of its vices, held by its pleasures, imprisoned in its exile, locked up in its body, nailed to its worries, distracted by its concerns, frozen by its fears, struck by manifold sufferings, going from error to error, eaten up by anxiety, ravaged by suspicion and, lastly, according to the prophet, a stranger in a foreign land ... , every soul, I say, in spite of its damnation and despair, can still find in itself reasons not only to hope for forgiveness and mercy but even to aspire to the wedding feast of the Word: as long as it does not fear to sign a covenant with God, and to place itself with him under the yoke of love. ... For the Bridegroom is not only a lover: he is Love. You will say: yes, but is he not also honour? Some affirm this; as to myself, I never read anything of that kind. I have read that God is Love."

[St. Bernard, Sermons sur Le Cantique des Cantiques, Sermon 83, (Paris, 1953), 846-848]

Chapter 5

The Dark Night of Love

The Canticle has its moments of darkness and confusion. All love stories are the same. In one of the poems we hear the lover knocks at the door of the bride:

> BELOVED: I sleep, but my heart is awake.
> I hear my love knocking.
> 'Open to me, my sister, my beloved,
> my dove, my perfect one.
> For my head is wet with dew,
> My hair with the drops of night.'
> - 'I have taken off my tunic,
> am I to put it on again?
> I have washed my feet,
> Am I to dirty them again?'
> My love thrust his hand
> Through the hole in the door;
> I trembled to the core of my being.
> *(Sg 5:2-4)*

It is now deepest night – the beloved is asleep but her love does not. Her lover comes in the cold of the night, his hair is wet with dew. The Book of the Apocalypse has a famous piece speaking of Jesus knocking at the door of the heart: "Behold, I stand at the door and knock. If anyone hears my voice and opens the door, I will come to him and dine with him and he with me" *(Rv 3:20)*.

But then there is a surprise!

> Then I got up
> to open to my love,
> myrrh ran off my hands,
> pure myrrh off my fingers,
> on to the handle of the bolt.

> I opened to my love,
> but he had turned and gone.
> My soul failed at his flight,
> I sought but could not find him,
> I called, but he did not answer.
>
> *(Sg 5:5-6)*

She has hesitated to get up – why? We do not know, but when she does – she finds her lover is gone. When she had heard the hand of her beloved on the door she had been deeply moved by love. The word used in Hebrew to indicate her love tells us that her inner being was moved by profound emotion. This same word is used in Hebrew to indicate womb or compassion, and is also the word used to indicate the maternal compassion of God *(see Jr 4:19, 31:20; Is 16:11, 49:15)*. Because she delays, however, the chance to meet her beloved seems to have gone.

Now she goes out into the city looking for her beloved. This was a brave thing for a woman at that time to do – so she is met with suspicion and even violence:

> The watchmen met me,
> those who go on their rounds in the city.
> They beat me, they wounded me,
> they took my cloak away from me:
> those guardians of the ramparts!
>
> I charge you,
> daughters of Jerusalem,
> if you should find my love,
> what are you to tell him?
> - That I am sick with love!
>
> *(Sg 5:7-8)*

The guards have here a symbolic function. They are impersonal and symbolize the brutality that threatens to destroy love. It could be from family *(1:6)*, authority *(8:11-12)*, society (one thinks of the chorus in *2:7,3:5*). The guards represent all those opposed to true love. The young girl in openly seeking this love doesn't conform to normal behaviour and therefore is rejected. She tells the chorus: "If you find my beloved, will you not tell him that I am faint with love" *(Sg 5:8)*. This is addressed to the chorus, the girls of Jerusalem who provide a kind of commentary on the love story. The Targum is an Aramaic translation and commentary on the book of the Bible. The Targum on the Song of Songs, *Midras Rabbah*, saw the sickness of love as speaking of Israel's lovesickness:

> The Assembly of Israel replied: "I adjure you, O prophets, by the decree of the Word of YHWH, if our love should appear to you, tell Him that I am sick from love of Him".
>
> *(Midras Rabbah)*

St. Augustine speaks of our restless hearts and that it's only in God that our hearts find rest.

> BELOVED: My love went down to his garden,
> To the beds of spices,
> To pasture his flock on the grass
> And gather lilies.
>
> I belong to my love, and my love to me.
> He pastures his flock among the lilies.
> *(Sg 6:2-3)*

Once again the poem in chapter 6 takes up the themes of new life, colour and flowers. She has found her lover again in his garden. Two poems now follow, one in praise of the lover *(Sg 6:4-12)* and the other a celebration of the loveliness of the beloved *(Sg 7:1-12)*. She has found her "journey's end in lover's meeting".

Earlier in the song the beloved had said:

> Catch the foxes for us,
> the little foxes
> that make havoc of the vineyards,
> for our vineyards are in flower.
> *(Sg 2:15)*

She hints here that the cause of love is never safe. In the Mediterranean basin the little foxes could destroy the garden. Love is precious and must be cultivated and cherished – she discovered this to her cost when she delayed in opening the door to her lover. The book of Deuteronomy gives a list of the wild animals that ravage the land *(Dt 20:17)*. The book of Lamentations describes the devastation of Jerusalem: "because Jerusalem is destroyed; jackals roam to and fro in it" *(Lm 5:18)*. As we saw Pope John Paul refers to the inner garden as that sacred part of our soul and the many 'foxes' can hurt that most intimate part.

Maurice Zundel and the "Secret Garden":

Maurice Zundel (1897-1975) was a Swiss born priest, a poet, philosopher, a theologian, and a mystic. He was quoted by Pope Paul VI in his encyclical *Popolorum Progressio*, and in 1971 gave the retreat to the Pope and the papal household. Pope Paul asked him to explore for him why people drifted from the faith. He tells the story of 'Little Henri' to answer this.

Maurice's career wasn't all a bed of roses – far from it. The "little foxes" did violate his sacred space but he did not despair. When he was a young man he found himself as a lone Catholic in a Protestant school, where he was treated with the utmost respect. All intolerance and bigotry were anathema to him after this. He made a friend in the school who influenced him for life. His friend introduced him to the Bible and especially the Beatitudes. These became precious to him. The two friends also developed a great love for literature.

One of the authors that was a favourite with the two youths was Victor Hugo. Hugo had a genius for showing great beauty even in the midst of misery. Maurice was very touched by Hugo's *Les Miserables*. Maurice took to heart the story of bishop Myriel and the escaped convict, Jean Valjean. The escaped convict stole two candlesticks belonging to the bishop. Valjean was arrested and the police brought him to the bishop Myriel. The bishop gave him the candlesticks – he told Valjean the church was the house of God and Valjean's too, so he was welcome to the candlesticks and he was to go with the bishop's blessing.

Later when Maurice was asked what happened to his friend, he replied with infinite sadness: "He took his life". Different things had happened to his sensitive friend that crushed his gentle spirit. That sacred part of him where God is present was not respected. This had a profound influence on Maurice. Maurice would remain poor for the rest of his life so that he could respect the sacred space, that secret garden, which is in each of us. An experience in the life of the writer Dostoevsky might help to illustrate Maurice's point. Dostoevsky on one of his travels had listened to a speech on equality. Later on at supper a poor man came to the hotel and Dostoevsky noted cynically that those who spoke of equality dined well while the poor man had to sing for his supper.

When Maurice was in Neuchatel he had a religious experience. He was praying before a status of Our Lady when he had an experience of love. He described the love of Mary as *Virgo Virginans*. By this he meant a love that possesses nothing, a love that is unconditional and which gives. He felt that love and felt called to give that love to others.

The Holy Spirit is the one who activates God's word and call in the human soul. Origen teaches that the Spirit brought forth Jesus in the Virgin's womb so that Jesus might equally be born in each Christian through the power of the same Spirit.

> What meaning does it have to say that Jesus has come only in the flesh which He received from Mary if I do not show He has come also in my flesh?
> *(Gn, hom III, 7)*

Again Origen insists that this overshadowing, as in Mary's case, is for us as well and we must want it as she did.

> ... and not only in Mary did this birth begin by the overshadowing of the Holy Spirit but in you also, if you are worthy of it, the Word of God is born. Then seek the ability to seize this overshadowing and when you will have been made worthy of this overshadowing, there will come to you through this overshadowing His body born in you.
> *(CC, hom III, 6)*

Mary brings to others the Holy Spirit and she continues to be a presence to all who ask her to come into their lives and make the rain of the Holy Spirit fall abundantly upon their thirsty, parched hearts. Jesus says in the Gospel of John: "Anyone who loves me will keep my word, and my Father will love him and we shall come to him and remain in him" *(Jn 14:23)*.

Maurice spoke later of the maternal love of Mary. He said it is incomparable and unique and envelops us totally. Her love reveals the maternal love of God because God is the source of all love. The love that is in Mary's heart comes from the very love that is in God's heart and which flows out to us through the Spirit. It reminds us that God is as much feminine as he is masculine. Mary reveals the maternal aspect of God's love *(Temoin d'une Presence, p.66)*. This love stayed with Maurice all his life.

When Maurice was a young priest he entered a long night of loneliness. His style of preaching was new and was resented by some. Jealousy was never far from him. He preached and practised poverty, which irritated a number of clerics who felt they were being criticized. More seriously there was a priest in his diocese, who had committed some misdemeanour, who accused Maurice in the wrong so as to save his own skin. This combination of circumstances forced Maurice to live more or less in exile for the rest of his life.

Georges Bernanos spoke of mediocre priests as being the great enemy within. They are like the "foxes" of the Song. Bernanos when he spoke of mediocrity was not, as far as I know, even aware of the great evil of clerical child-abuse. Maurice knew of both the jealousy and mediocrity of so many priests, but he was resolved never to hurt the inner space of any person, no matter how much he disapproved of their actions. He set himself to live this vocation even in spite of the fact that he himself had been hurt badly. He was like the girl in the Canticle who while seeking love had suffered at the hands of the violent. He resolved to meet all, including the mediocre and downright malicious, with love beyond all telling.

Maurice's Teaching:

Maurice spent his life preaching and teaching. His friends were initially the poor but his holiness reached out to all. His love healed many souls and one of his devotees was the man who would become Pope Paul VI – monsignor Montini. Pope Paul VI would quote Maurice's teaching on the dignity of each person in his 1967 encyclical, *Popolorum Progressio*. Maurice was very influenced by the person of St. Francis – he wished to imitate St. Francis in the life of poverty he lived and in giving generously. One of Maurice's favourite poets was Rimbaud and he was fond of quoting this line from Rimbaud: "Je est un autre" (roughly translated it means "I am (is) the other"). The heart of the statement means that it is only in relationships that I become truly myself.

During his lifetime his followers began to collect together his thoughts and continued this work after his death. Thanks to their work we still have access to Maurice's teaching on the secret garden, that is, the sacred part of our souls. He was influenced in his approach by Blaise Pascal who said that there was an infinite distance between the flesh and the Spirit, and that there was also still an infinite distance between our spirit and true love. In his teachings a human being is not something readymade but we are all a someone we are meant to become. We are on a journey to the centre of our soul where God, who is Love, lives.

He was fond of quoting a Swiss-German writer of the 19th century called Gottfried Keller. Maurice quotes an episode from a novel by Keller, said to be autobiographical, called *Heinrich der Grune*:

> Little Henri was the only child of a widowed mother; she did her best to bring him up and lavished her tender love on him. He was eight or nine years old at the time. He came home from school one late afternoon; his supper was waiting for him and he sat down at the table without, for the first time, saying grace. His mother, taking this to be a moment of absent-mindedness, gently drew his attention to the omission. He pretended not to hear. She insisted. He stiffened in silent resistance. Then, in a

commanding tone, his mother said: "You do not want to say your prayer? – No! – Well then, go to bed without your supper!" The child bravely took up the challenge and went to bed without saying a word. Some time later, the mother, racked with remorse, brought him supper in bed. Too late: from that moment on, the little boy ceased to pray.

This minor incident is heavy with meaning. It makes us see a child becoming aware of his inviolability as a person. He discovers within himself a place his mother cannot enter without his consent, his own personal domain of which he alone can dispose. To be sure, he would be at a loss to define it, but he has such a keen perception of it that, henceforth, he will give up praying in order to constantly maintain, against his mother's infringement, its intangible independence.

(Inner Person, p.39)

Henri revolted against this invasion of his inner space and in many ways down through the ages this revolt is repeated in many different ways by groups trodden underfoot. In *Macbeth*, Shakespeare moves the crowd to see how hard it is to be true to that inner self and become the person one is called to be.

The main character of this tragedy is, as you know, Lady Macbeth, ambition personified. Her only goal is to attain the highest rank and enjoy the honours attached to it. In Scotland, where she lives, the highest honour is to wear the crown. Since witches have predicted that her husband will become king, she is consumed with the desire to hasten the fulfillment of this omen. There is only one obstacle: the reigning king. If he disappears, the throne will fall to Macbeth by right and she will be queen. Under her spell, Macbeth murders the king, his host, and lays the crime on the guards at the door of the royal chamber. The true murderers accede to the throne according to their plan. At the height of her glory, Lady Macbeth revels in the homages paid to her, relishing the kind of divinity that supreme power implies for her.

But in order to consolidate the benefits of his first crime, Macbeth is forced to commit a series of other crimes. These can no longer be concealed, and the usurpers are unmasked. The truth is revealed, and soon Lady Macbeth reads nothing but hatred and contempt in the eyes of the courtiers, who are waiting for the right moment to overthrow the murderous couple. She is the first to understand this: no one believes in her royalty any more. How could she believe in it herself, since it was from the eyes of others that she derived the image of her greatness. All her dreams collapse and she is left with nothing.

The external world she wanted to conquer and possess escapes her. And for her, the inner world does not exist and can offer her neither a refuge nor the chance to recreate herself. She has no access to her innermost self, buried as it is under a passion-driven ego, completely turned outward and with which she has totally identified. Disconnected from the two facets of being, she can no longer survive anywhere.

So she goes mad and thinks she sees on her hands the blood of the victims sacrificed to her ambition. Blood on her hands, not on her conscience, which could be the first step towards a liberating repentance. She wears herself out desperately trying to rub off the incriminating stain. "Out, out, damned spot!" But it persists and, no longer able to stand the sight of it, Lady Macbeth kills herself.
(The Inner Self, p.43f)

How do we find the inner person? Maurice used the story of the woman at the well from the Gospel of John *(Jn 4:5-30)* where Jesus asks the woman for a drink, and tells her he can offer her living water. He tells her that this living water can turn into a spring inside her, the spring of the Holy Spirit, welling up to eternal life. The woman had come to the well at a quiet time of the day presumably to avoid people. This is perhaps because people disapprove of the way she lives her life and show their disapproval by being unkind to her. We know from her conversation with Jesus that she has had five husbands and that the man she has now is not her husband. Regardless of what she may have done in the past, however, Jesus treats the woman with love and respect and wants to offer her the water of new life in the Spirit. He tells her that the kind of worshippers the Father wants are those who worship in spirit and truth *(Jn 4:24)*.

We are incapable on our own of justifying the respect for our honour that we look for.
Maurice says we must look for a solid basis for our most fundamental claims. We must look for the place of encounter, within ourselves, with the presence that moves us to go from a narcissistic monologue to the dialogue of love. Maurice speaks of how God's presence is brought to mind through literature, art and science but following St. Augustine he says this presence is found at the centre of our being where God is closer to us than we are to ourselves.

> "Late I came to love you, O Beauty, so ancient and so new; I came to love you late. You were inside and I was outside, rushing about, frantically searching for you like some monster let loose in your beautiful world. You were with me, but I was not with you."
> *(Augustine, Confessions, X)*

It is in the quiet moments of prayer that we discover who we are in relationship with God and it is in this context that Maurice sees prayer and revelation. Maurice says Christianity is less a doctrine and more a person – the very person of Jesus *(Je est un Autre, p.75)*. Revelation leads us to the presence of the person. "God is relation" and the Spirit unites us in that relationship.

Maurice was moved by Saint Francis and he had a unique insight into Francis and Lady Poverty. "St. Francis discovered, in his poverty, the fulfillment of all his ambitions. He had dreams of glory, and he desired to conquer the world ... he understood at Spoleto, that that was too little for him…Then, he found he could conquer the world in a different way and that he could love the world freely in the total offering that he would make of himself" *(Croyez Vous en Homme, p.24)*. Saint Francis renounced all possessions and gave himself totally to God. He spoke of marrying Lady Poverty. Maurice said Lady Poverty was another name for God. God was totally poor because he was totally generous. This was most clearly revealed in Jesus' birth into poverty and his lonely death on the cross. He loved his own even to the point of death and abandonment. We are called to open ourselves to this love and become united with God in making people aware of their dignity as temples of the Holy Spirit *(1 Co 6:19)*. This is where we find true healing and love. St. Theophane the Recluse said that prayer is a journey from the head to the heart (that inner core of our being) where God lives.

In one of his talks on Our Lady, Maurice meditates on the line in St. Paul's letter to the Philippians where Paul says that for him to live is Christ *(Ph 1:21)*:

> "This is a little compendium, at once brief and dense, of the Christian life. To live, is someone."

To allow Christ to live in us is the object of 'maternity'. "Anyone who does the will of God, that person is my brother and sister and mother' *(Mk 3:35)*. This is what Maurice means by maternity –becoming Christ-like in our being.

The prologue of John's gospel says that the light was not welcomed by the darkness, that the light was in the world but was not recognized by the world, that he came among his own but was not welcome. As the prologue indicates we are free to reject Christ and to reject becoming like him. To become Christ-like, or as Maurice puts it, 'divine maternity', is something we are free to choose or not to choose, and it is for this reason that Maurice says that God is fragile:

> God is fragile, God is infinite fragility.
> God is in danger of death.
> God has an essential need of us.
> *(Maria-Tenerezza di Dio, p.68)*

God is love but the darkness too is real. Mary radiated to Maurice the tenderness of God's love. Jesus gave his life so that we might experience God's love and so that this love might find a home in us. As Maurice says in his dramatic poem, God is once more in danger of death – he might still be rejected.

Chapter 6

Dare We Hope

Hope is something of a forgotten virtue. We live in a world where there is much violence, rejection and abuse. To reject someone is tantamount to killing them – so when it comes to celebrating a song of love we can feel we are gazing at the unattainable. Here I think of the idea of the Russian icon. There is often a bright gold colour that permeates the icon – in this way the artist shows us the way God's light is there. The people who prayed and those who painted the icons often lived harsh, hard lives. The icon represented the hope they held out that one day the light would transform the darkness. I find the same when I meditate on the Song of Songs.

After the beloved has been found, the lover composes this poem in her honour. It is in the form of *wasf*, ancient Middle East love poetry in which the beauty of the beloved is portrayed. By meditating on the picture of love we hope to one day let that love in:

LOVER: You are fair as Tirzah, my beloved,
        enchanting as Jerusalem,
        formidable as an army!
        Turn your eyes away from me,
        they take me by assault!
        Your hair is like a flock of goats
        surging down the slopes of Gilead.
        Your teeth are like a flock of ewes
        as they come up from being washed.
        Each one has its twin,
        not one unpaired with another.
        Your cheeks, behind your veil,
        are halves of pomegranate.

        There are sixty queens
        and eighty concubines
        (and countless girls).

> My dove is my only one,
> perfect and mine.
> She is the darling of her mother,
> the favourite of the one who bore her.
> Girls have seen her and proclaimed her blessed,
> queens and concubines have sung her praises,
> 'Who is this arising like the dawn,
> fair as the moon,
> resplendent as the sun,
> formidable as an army?'
>
> I went down to the nut orchard
> to see the fresh shoots in the valley,
> to see if the vines were budding
> and the pomegranate trees in flower.
> Before I knew ... my desire had hurled me
> onto the chariots of Amminadib!
>
> *(Sg 6:4-12)*

The lover responds to the beloved, first by returning to the theme of her incomparable beauty *(vv 4-10)*, and then by acknowledging the power she has over him *(vv 11-12)*. The author of the book of Proverbs had meditated on the power of love over the heart of a man:

> Three things are too wonderful for me;
> > four I do not understand:
> the way of an eagle in the sky,
> > the way of a snake on a rock,
> the way of a ship on the high seas,
> > and the way of a man with a girl.
>
> *(Pr 30:18-19)*

The lover describes his beloved in terms that make us think she is most wonderful to behold. In verse 4 her beauty is compared with that of Tirzah and Jerusalem. Tirzah was the first capital of the northern kingdom of Israel. She is compared to the beauty of the great capital cities, only more precious. It is like in Shakespeare's *Romeo and Juliet* where we hear:

> "But, soft! What light through yonder window breaks?
> It is the east and Juliet is the sun"

The last two verses *(vv 11-12)* pick up a thought already expressed in verse 5. He imagines himself coming to his garden of love *(see 5:1)*. It is springtime, the time of awakening life. The lover is overcome. The last verse 12 is generally considered the hardest to translate – so a quick look at the varieties of approaches can be used to get the sense of the passage:

> RSV – Before I was aware, my fancy set me
> in a chariot beside my prince.
>
> GNB – I am trembling; you have made me
> as eager for love
> as a chariot driver is for battle.
>
> NEB – I did not know myself;
> she made me feel more than a prince
> reigning over the myriads of his people.

Then all of a sudden we hear the chorus call the Shulamite woman. They refer to a dance that we in our time do not know:

> CHORUS: Come back, come back, girl from Shulam,
> come back, come back, where we can look at you!
> Why are you looking at the girl from Shulam,
> dancing between two lines of dancers?
>
> *(Sg 7:1)*

The maidens who form the chorus seem to say: "Let us see for ourselves what the lover sees in the Shulamite woman". The girl from Shulam seems to say: "Why look at me as if I was different?" She has been prepared to challenge anyone who tries to rebuff her sense of self *(see 1:5, 8:10)*. She asserts her identity and dignity as a person and this is her response to the *wasf* of the lover. He shows his acceptance of this correction by continuing with another *wasf* in praise of his beloved:

> How beautiful are your feet in their sandals,
> O prince's daughter!
> The curve of your thighs is like the curve of a necklace,
> work of a master hand.
> Your navel is a bowl well rounded
> with no lack of wine,
> your belly a heap of wheat
> surrounded with lilies.
> Your two breasts are two fawns,
> twins of a gazelle.
> Your neck is an ivory tower.
> Your eyes, the pools of Heshbon,
> by the gate of Bath-Rabbim.
> Your nose, the Tower of Lebanon,
> sentinel facing Damascus.
> Your head is held high like Carmel,
> and its hair is as dark as purple;
> a king is held captive in your tresses.
>
> *(Sg 7:2-6)*

Her nose is compared to Lebanon which guards the East. Lebanon in Hebrew also means white. Then she is compared to Carmel (this literally translates as the vineyard of God or the fertile vine par-excellence). He is held captive by the love he has for the woman.

Choraqui in his commenting on the Canticle, meditates on the dance *(Le Cantique des Cantiques, p.72)*:

"The chorus contemplates in the Bride the dance, i.e., the dynamic harmony of reconciled opposites. The two camps that were enemies yesterday – with the hardships of separation and exile – are now reconciled in the reflection of triumphant love. ... Love reconciles the opposites, resolves them in its cosmic dance, reflected by the maid of Shulam returning from exile and being wed again. ... She must appear in the eyes of creation so that the latter might be fulfilled in the contemplation of a reconciled universe, re-created to the image of the couple who is triumphant in the unity of love. Yes, a dance and no more a war of the two camps. ... The maid of Shulam continues to bear in her womb two camps that are now pacified in the new rhythm of their cosmic dance."

Charles Péguy – Prophet of Hope:

Charles Péguy (1873-1914) was one of France's best-loved poets. His influence spread to such people as Bernanos, Marcel, Guardini, de Lubac and Balthasar. He was born in Orleans. His father died the year Charles was born following wounds he received in the Franco-Prussian war. Charles was always devoted to the maid of Orleans, Joan of Arc.

When Charles was a young man he became disenchanted with Christianity as he found it. He was troubled by the doctrine of Hell or more so by the ready way in which people were prepared to condemn others to Hell and gloat over their misery. Saint Silouan the Athonite (1886-1938) shared this view with Péguy. Silouan prayed all the time and developed a sense of universal compassion. This is what the young Péguy did not find among his fellow Christians. Péguy also saw the living hell on earth that so many people had to suffer. He saw the exploitation of the workers and the lack of social justice. Again he saw no compassion – no care. He became involved in the notorious Dreyfus affair. Dreyfus was Jewish officer wrongly tried and convicted. This injustice greatly offended Péguy and he joined with such souls as Zola and Jaures to fight for the man's cause. Péguy remarked that if we allow injustice to one man then we allow it happen to all. Leon Bloy (1846-1917) remarked that Christian anti-Semitism was one of the greatest wounds inflicted on Jesus because these were his people

In 1905 Charles founded the *Cahiers de la Quinzaine*, a magazine to argue for his message. During this time, too, he announced quietly to a few friends that he had found faith again. He told his friend Joseph Lotte in 1908: "I am a Catholic". Because his wife and family did not want to convert he found himself temporarily away from the sacraments. During this time, too, he fell in love with another woman other than his wife. This was a time of great tribulation for him but he never did anything inappropriate or betrayed his natural family. He was called up on the outbreak of the Great War. He was one of the first killed at the front but he had received the sacraments a few days beforehand and was at peace. During his life he wrote many plays and poems. He had great devotion to Our Lady, whom he call "all hope". She had played a secret part in his conversion and he wrote beautifully about her in his poetry. He often undertook a pilgrimage from Paris to Chartres in her honour and he confided all his many problems to her. He wrote once that it was sad that the same spirit of criticism that was used against religion did not find a similar expression in such areas as economics, poetry, human rights and politics. What would he have said in an age of nuclear-proliferation, the destruction of the planet, global poverty, lack of care, and the easy-way in which states go to war and the innocent suffer? What would he say in a world of spin and deceit where gall is king?

Péguy's Meditations:

Ugo Vanni studied the book of the Apocalypse. In it he sees the final destruction of evil where the good co-operate with Jesus in the final victory. The final victory is described in the description of the new Jerusalem:

> Then I saw *a new heaven and a new earth*; the first heaven and the first earth had disappeared now, and there was no longer any sea. I saw the holy city, the new Jerusalem, coming down out of heaven from God, prepared as a bride dressed for her husband. Then I heard a loud voice call from the throne, 'Look, here God lives among human beings. He will make *his home among them; they will be his people*, and he will be their God, *God-with-them. He will wipe* away all *tears from their eyes*; there will be no more death, and no more mourning or sadness or pain. The world of the past has gone.'
>
> Then the One sitting on the throne spoke. 'Look, I am making the whole of creation new.'
> *(Rv 21:1-5)*

This passage shows the hope of a new creation where all tears are wiped away, all is light. The days of darkness are over and we will live in peace with God.

The new Jerusalem is described in chapter 19 as a bride coming from heaven:

> Then a voice came from the throne; it said, 'Praise our God, you servants of his and *those who fear him, small and great alike.*' And I heard what seemed to be the voices of a huge crowd, like the sound of the ocean or the great roar of thunder, answering, 'Alleluia! The reign of the Lord our God Almighty has begun; let us be glad and joyful and give glory to God, because this is the time for the marriage of the Lamb. His bride is ready, and she has been able to dress herself in dazzling white linen, because her linen is made of the good deeds of the saints.' The angel said, 'Write this, "Blessed are those who are invited to the wedding feast of the Lamb,"' and he added, 'These words of God are true.' Then I knelt at his feet to worship him, but he said to me, 'Never do that: I am your fellow-servant and the fellow-servant of all your brothers who have in themselves the witness of Jesus. God alone you must worship.' The witness of Jesus is the spirit of prophecy.
> *(Rv 19:5-10)*

The interesting line is *19:8* where the dress of the Bride is the goodness of those who have the Spirit of Jesus. The new creation is built by Jesus and those who work with him. It is the author's way of saying that our good deeds, our acts of loving, the witness of the martyrs is of eternal value and the new creation is dressed in these deeds. Looking at things without God the just seem to disappear but in the eye of God they are the ones who build the new world. Love is eternal and is stronger than death.

Charles Péguy was moved by the Spirit. He did not say things in the same way as the Book of the Apocalypse, but the teachings of both complement each other. Both were moved by the same Holy Spirit of God.

Péguy reflected on the person of Jesus in all his mysteriousness. The centre of Christianity was for him "A Man God, a God man" *(Veronique, p.397)*. The hidden life of Jesus was important for him too. It was at Nazareth he grew to maturity with Mary and Joseph. The quiet love he learned and practised there prepared him for his public life. Péguy believed that every wound we inflict on Jesus is an eternal wound. We do this by our injustice *(Veronique, p.383)* but Jesus has come to lead us to new life in him, away from the way of hurt to the way of love. Christianity has placed 'the infinite everywhere'.

The agony of Jesus has an infinite dimension, because of the infinite person Jesus is, who takes to himself the sins of the world. The infinity of Jesus' sufferings is revealed firstly in the agony in Gethsemane, and finally in the cry of abandonment on the Cross. Péguy said we too often forget Good Friday racing from Palm Sunday to Easter day.

> "You do not hear any more across the centuries or generations the echo of that sad agony, more than infinitely sad … The echo, the annual echo, the ritual echo, the solemn echo of the sadness of the just, of so much suffering, of an infinite suffering …"
> *(Veronique. p.445)*

Yet in the end Jesus overcame death and he leads from death to life those who come to him.

> "That will was done. The light was made, the light that existed in the beginning has come again. As the light was made once, now for the second time with the doing of God's will the light has come a second time."
> *(Veronique, p.476)*

It is the vision of the Book of the Apocalypse – all things are being made new. In Péguy's next work *Jeanne d'Arc* he shows us how Jeanne abandons herself into the hands of God accepting even dereliction and seeming loss of God. She offers herself to God to cooperate with him in his final victory. Jesus' agony continues across the centuries. There are those who know Jesus by the light that shines in their hearts without being able to name him. Péguy always respected these people.

In 1911 Péguy published *The Portal of the Mystery of Hope*. This is my favourite work of Péguy. Péguy tells us that Jesus' words were pronounced "carnally" in time: we are to give flesh to his words just as Mary gave flesh to the child in her womb. The work of the incarnation will not be complete, says Péguy, until the whole of creation is assumed – all of time, all of the finite, all of the carnal, every sinner must be taken up into God's life. God wishes to be glorified in every aspect of creation, but it is in hope that he is best glorified, for it is in hope that a person most profoundly expresses the greatest trust in God, the greatest confidence in God's love. The child becomes a central image in the *Portal*, because the child is absolute helplessness and dependence, is one who "smiles inwardly", with the complete assurance of being borne along by the parents' love. This reminds us of Jesus' love for children *(see Mk 9:37, 10:13-17 et passim)*. To hope means to recognize the boundless grace of God as the reality that surrounds and affects us, the reality in which we bathe and remake our being, the reality that accompanies us in our "greatest follies" and in "the shamefulness of our sins", unceasingly reminding us that God's love for us remains constant despite our inconsistency. Every person who hopes in God represents God's own truth. Every time we love and hope we bring God's eternity into the present. Love is God's very being. I am reminded here of the painter Georges Roualt (1871-1958). He shows us the lonely and despised in his paintings, but yet they all held out hope for redemption. Jesus is found with the despised and lonely. In one of Roualt's pictures of the suffering face of Jesus, we see a face of infinite sadness yet the face is bathed with light showing us the hope that love will overcome death and the new creation will be a reality *(see Rv 22:1-5)*.

> According to Péguy, God, too, is joined with his creatures in hoping: He has entered into creation out of love, and asks his creature to respond in love, and this means in freedom. Since freedom is essential to love, God cannot force himself on the one he loves. Instead, he himself is forced to await the

freedom of his creature, forced to "hope for the sinner". But, nevertheless, God does not stand apart, waiting passively for this freedom. He has gone out to meet his creature, he has truly "taken the initiative" – indeed, as Péguy says elsewhere, God has "sacrificed everything to obtain this freedom." This "sacrifice" that God makes in his supreme hope for the sinner once again reveals the glory of his love, and it does so by way of a paradox, for it is precisely the omnipotence of God's love that allows him to risk the humiliation and powerlessness of the Crucifixion.

Péguy's vision of hope manifests itself in the peculiarity of his poetic style. As another French writer, Romain Rolland, has said of Péguy, "I know of no other writer who has ever made God speak in such a manner." It is undoubtedly the colloquial character of Péguy's idiom that first strikes us as unusual. In the Portal, God speaks to us as a merciful, as a hopeful, Father, who tries to elicit hope from his creatures. His language is filled with images drawn from the basic experiences of life, rather than sophisticated argumentation aimed at an elite few. There is not a trace of condescension in his tone: God does not speak from the sublime heights of heaven, looking down at the world from an infinite distance. Rather, having assumed everything human, he speaks from within the world; he speaks, as it were, as "one of us." Like an old French peasant, he is absolutely serious about what he is saying, and yet an affectionate humour pervades every sentence. His manner is gentle and compassionate, and yet always firm. But what is perhaps most remarkable in Péguy's style is that the familiar tone of God's speech never compromises God's infinite greatness. We never once forget that God is the Creator, and if he does not speak from infinitely above us, it is only because he himself has crossed the distance out of his gratuitous love. What Péguy says in the poem of the Blessed Virgin can therefore also be said, inversely, of God: He makes himself infinitely lowly precisely because he is infinitely lofty. And so, Péguy's profound insight into the nature of God's love is carried all the way through into the style of speech that communicates it.

Finally, Péguy's insistence on the incarnational nature of God's love reveals itself in the fact that God speaks, in the *Portal*, through a concrete character in a drama. The *Portal* is not just a long free-verse poem uttered from "out of the blue"; rather, as the title suggests, it is in fact a play. The "portal" refers to the entranceway of medieval cathedrals, whose tympana often depicted a Christian mystery. The cathedral's portal was also where Christian mystery plays were typically enacted. If we keep in mind that the *Portal* is a play, we are better able to appreciate the conversational quality of the writing. Madame Gervaise, God's "mouthpiece" in the poem, addresses her monologue to the young Joan of Arc, who remains silent throughout. She speaks in short phrases, pausing after each one as if to make sure that "Jeannette" has understood it. And, as in any conversation, Madame Gervaise often digresses from a thought, only to pick it up again several lines – or even pages! – later. These long pauses, along with the constant repetition of a word or phrase, create a slow, meditative rhythm. The rhythm, however, never becomes heavy, because each repetition adds a new dimension, and so deepens the meditation at every turn.

Thus, all of the elements of Péguy's work – his concrete images, his colloquial idiom, his striking insights into the heart of God – gather together into a single, powerful statement of the central place of hope in the Christian life. And it is unlikely that anyone who has heard this "word of hope" will ever again be able to silence it in his or her heart.

(see Schindler, preface to 'Portal', XX-XXII)

Extracts from the Poem:

The Portal itself is a long poem, so I propose just to share a few passages that speak to me. In the poem we hear God say that hope surprises him. Péguy once complained that we do not hear or listen to the voice of God. In his own life he once tried not to listen but he returned to God and in spite of many difficulties learned to hope. We hear God say:

But hope, says God, that is something that surprises me.
Even me.
That is surprising.
That these poor children see how things are going and believe that tomorrow things will go better.
That they see how things are going today and believe that they will go better tomorrow morning.
That is surprising and it's by far the greatest marvel of our grace.
And I'm surprised by it myself.
And my grace must indeed be an incredible force,
And must flow freely and like an inexhaustible river.
Since the first time it flowed and since it has forever been flowing.
In my natural and supernatural creation.
In my spiritual and carnal and yet spiritual creation.
In my eternal and temporal and yet eternal creation.
Mortal and immortal.

There is so much that militates against hope in our world – yet in the midst of despair there often comes someone who re-ignites our hope – it can be a saint, a poet, or maybe an artist. I think of the effect of listening to the song The Rose where love seems lost yet in the spring blooms again. Hope against hope is a great miracle.

What surprises me, says God, is hope.
And I can't get over it.
This little hope who seems like nothing at all.
This little girl hope.
Immortal.

Because my three virtues, says God.
The three virtues, my creatures.
My daughters, my children.
Are themselves like my other creatures.
Of the race of men.
Faith is a loyal Wife.
Charity is a Mother.

> An ardent mother, noble-hearted.
> Or an older sister who is like a mother.
> Hope is a little girl, nothing at all.
> Who came into the world on Christmas day just this past year.

Jesus came as a defenseless child who was rejected and died. He is the face in Roualt's painting, infinitely sad. He is the Jesus of Pascal whose suffering continues in the sufferings of every person until the end of time. Their tears "are the tears of the child" who hopes because God's love is more powerful than death and leads us through death to new life.

The central mystery of Christianity is the incarnation. According to the traditional adage of the Fathers of the Church, God truly became man so that we could truly become God. All mistrust of the flesh, all hatred of the temporal, is therefore an abomination, for it is a mistrust and hatred of the very real conditions that the Word has assumed in order to redeem them. God so loved the world – and not only souls, but bodies, the earth, creation – that he sent his only Son.

One creature is the prototype of the new humanity redeemed by Christ: Mary, the mother of Jesus. She is superior both to humans and to angels, because while she is carnal like humans, she is also pure like the angels, without the shadow of sin. She alone is a perfect imitation of Jesus, because she alone is wholly terrestrial and wholly divinized. Péguy's devotion to Mary, far from being an overly devout pietism, is an exultation of the temporal by the eternal, and a glorification of the flesh by the spirit.

In the poem Péguy speaks of the woodcutter who brings his sick children to Mary, because she is the unique intercessor. She is "hope" itself. This is autobiographical in that Péguy is here referring to himself.

> His three children in sickness, in the misery where they lay.
> And he had peacefully given them to you.
> In prayer he had given them to you.
> Placed very peacefully within the arms of she who bears all of

> the world's sufferings.
> And whose arms are already so full.
> Because the Son has taken away all sins.
> But the Mother has taken away all suffering.

Péguy's picture of Mary is influenced by St. John's picture of her at the foot of the Cross of her son. There she stands with the beloved disciple *(Jn 19:25-27)*. Jesus breathes out his Spirit on this community and they become his Spirit bearers to the world. Mary sees the death of her son and now she shares the tears of all Jesus' brothers and sisters, whose mother she has become, too. Her son took away all sins, she bears all our tears.

So then the 'woodcutter' takes his courage in his hands and presents the sick ones to Mary, to "she who intercedes".

> And so you must gather your courage with both hands.
> And address yourself directly to she who is above them all.
> Be bold. Just once. Address yourself boldly to she who is infinitely beautiful.
> Because she's also infinitely good.
>
> To she who intercedes.
> The only one who can speak with the authority of a mother.
> Address yourself boldly to she who is infinitely pure.
> Because she's also infinitely gentle.
>
> To she who is infinitely noble.
> Because she's also infinitely gracious.
> Infinitely courteous.
> Courteous like the priest who at the threshold of the church
> goes to meet the newborn at the threshold.
> On the day of his baptism.
> To introduce him into the house of God.
>
> To she who is infinitely rich.
> Because she's also infinitely poor.

> To she who is infinitely lofty.
> Because she's also infinitely lowly.
>
> To she who is infinitely great.
> Because she's also infinitely small.
> Infinitely humble.
> A young mother.
>
> To she who is infinitely righteous.
> Because she's also infinitely yielding.
>
> To she who is infinitely joyful.
> Because she's also infinitely sorrowful.

This page is autobiographical because as he admitted privately his devotion to Mary enabled him to return to a deeper faith and new hope. Our tears are God's. Mary shows us the maternal love of God. As St. Maximilian Kolbe says "the Holy Spirit is the Immaculate Conception" and Mary is uniquely united with God's Holy Spirit. In this Spirit she is one with the tears of humanity praying all the time that those tears be transformed and we find our home in the New Jerusalem where every tear will be wiped away.

Péguy goes on to develop his theme of hope. Mary has led him to God. Now he reflects on the hope of God. He tells us:

> You must have confidence in God, he certainly has had confidence in us.
> You must trust God, he certainly has put his trust in us.
> You must hope in God, he has certainly hoped in us.
> You must give God a chance, he has certainly given us a chance.
> What chance.
> Every chance.
> You must have faith in God, he certainly has faith in us.

God sees the good in each of us. He knows there is sinfulness but he has come that we might die to sinfulness. He has come that we might have life and have it to the full *(Jn 10:10)*. Péguy shows the faith and hope God has in us. He repeats:

> It's God who gave us a chance, who put his trust in us.
> Who gave us credence, who had faith in us.
> Will this confidence be misplaced, will it be said that this confidence was misplaced.
> God put his hope in us. He took the initiative. He hoped that the least of the sinners,
> That the tiniest of the sinners would at least work a little for his own salvation.
> Just a little, as poorly as it might be.
> That he would look after it a bit.
> He hoped in us, will it be said that we didn't hope in him.
> God placed his hope, his poor hope in each one of us, in the tiniest of the sinners. Will it be said that we tiny ones, that we sinners will it be we who do not place our hope in him.

Péguy complained that we do not know or hear the word of God. He tries in his poetry to open our eyes and ears to the love that is around us and there to see the love of God revealed in the Word made flesh *(Jn 1:14)*. The Word of God is ultimately a word of love for each of us.

> The word of God is not a tangled ball of yarn.
> It's a beautiful woolen thread which winds itself around the spindle.
> As he spoke to us, thus we ought to listen.
> As he spoke to Moses.
> As he spoke to us through Jesus.
> As he spoke to us all, thus we ought to listen.
>
> Yes, my child, if that's how it is, if it's like this that we ought to listen to Jesus.
> That we ought to listen to God.

Etty Hillesum (1914-1943) was a Dutch Jewess who embodies for me Péguy's idea of God's hope in us. She always reminds me of the beloved Shulamite woman of the Canticle. She didn't in any way conform to normal patterns – as the Shulamite woman defied all conventions, so in her own way did Etty. She went through many torrid love affairs and suffered deeply from depression.

Her therapist led her to read her Bible and pray. She would spend a length of time in the morning (usually in the bathroom!) where she would reflect on the torments in her soul. Then later she would pray and meditate. She became very attached to the Gospel of St. Matthew – she was moved by the figure of Jesus who gave his broken body so that others might have life. She also discovered deep in the centre of her being that there God lived. In this way she learned to like herself – the grace of graces. We cannot love others unless we love ourselves and it was in finding that God is closer to us than we are to ourselves that Etty learned to love herself and others. She saw her mission in life, in the face of the world at war and the annihilation of her people, to find a love for God in people's hearts. This was the only protest she could make against the hatred of the Nazis and the extinction of the Jewish people. She said that it was now God who needed us and she gave herself to him.

She was taken to Auschwitz concentration camp. She did have an opportunity to escape, but like Jesus giving his broken body, she felt called to give her broken body so that some would die with hope. In the midst of all that was indecent and ugly she was determined to carry the spark of God's love and show people it dwelt in their hearts. This light can never be put out by human hatred. She died in Auschwitz at the age of 29. Her diary and letters haven given many hope, as she did with the giving of her life.

I am especially fond of the last entry into her diary. She had always found solace in the poetry of Rilke and the beauty of his verse had given her great hope. It was his verse that alerted her at an earlier stage that there is "something else out there" – he led her to find God.

> I have broken my body like bread and shared it out among men. And why not, they were hungry and had gone without for so long.
> I always return to Rilke. It is strange to think that

someone so frail, who did most of his writing within protective castle walls, would perhaps have been broken by the circumstances in which we now live. Is that not further testimony that life is finely balanced? Evidence that, in peaceful times and under favourable circumstances, sensitive artists may search for the purest and most fitting expression of their deepest insights so that, during more turbulent and debilitating times, others can turn to them for support and a ready response to their bewildered questions? A response they are unable to formulate for themselves, since all their energies are taken up in looking after the bare necessities? Sadly, in difficult times we tend to shrug off the spiritual heritage of artists from an easier age (yet isn't an artist always difficult in fact?) with a scornful "What is that sort of thing to us now?"

It is an understandable but shortsighted reaction. And utterly impoverishing.

We should be willing to act as a balm for all wounds.

(Tuesday 13th Oct, 1942)

Chapter 7

Love, A Flame of Yahweh Himself

The psalmist in *Psalm 16* says: "I said: Yahweh, my Lord, you are my good, above you there is no other" *(16:2)*. The Hindu mystic Turkaram along the same lines says: "May he be your unique God: without him there is no joy for you. You are my all, my only one. In every stone I see you. In my soul there is no more anguish". All love leads to the source of love. The Canticle is composed, as we said, of love poetry and while it's only in chapter 8 that the divine name Yahweh (in the shortened form Yah) is mentioned, he has been present throughout. Dostoevsky once said: " What is hell? I affirm it is the torment of not being able to love anymore". The end of chapter 7 and the beginning of chapter 8 go as follows:

> THE BRIDE   Wine flowing straight to my Beloved,
> as it runs on the lips of those who sleep,
> I am my Beloved's,
> and his desire is for me.
> Come, my Beloved,
> let us go to the fields.
> We will spend the night in the villages,
> and in the morning we will go to the vineyards.
> We will see if the vines are budding,
> if their blossoms are opening,
> if the pomegranate trees are in flower.
> Then I shall give you
> the gift of my love.
> The mandrakes yield their fragrance,
> the rarest fruits are at our doors;
> the new as well as the old,
> I have stored them for you, my Beloved.
>
> Ah, why are you not my brother,
> nursed at my mother's breast!
> Then if I met you out of doors, I could kiss you

without people thinking ill of me.
I should lead you, I should take you
into my mother's house, and you would teach me!
I should give you spiced wine to drink,
juice of my pomegranates.
His left arm is under my head
and his right embraces me.

THE BRIDEGROOM
I charge you,
daughters of Jerusalem,
not to stir my love, nor rouse it,
until it please to awake.
(7:10 - 8:4)

She accepts the invitation of the beloved and she comes to him. The symbol of the mandrake shows she is ready for love. She longs for the day when she may openly profess their love so that the entire world will know of it. She wishes she could take his love to her mother's house. Chapter 8 verses *3-4* repeat *2:6-7*. There is no longer, however, any reference to "the gazelles or the hinds of the field". Also in *2:7* and *3:5* the words are in the form of an order. "[I charge you] ... that you stir not nor waken ...". There is no longer any need to plead their love be allowed to take its natural course. Once she has brought him home and their relationship is there for all the world to acknowledge, she defies anyone to interfere.

CONCLUSION

THE CHORUS   Who is this coming up from the desert
leaning on her Beloved?

THE BRIDEGROOM
I awakened you under the apple tree,
there where your mother conceived you,
there where she who gave birth to you conceived you.
Set me like a seal on your heart,

> like a seal on your arm.
> For love is strong as Death,
> jealousy relentless as Sheol.
> The flash of it is a flash of fire,
> a flame of Yahweh himself.
> Love no flood can quench,
> no torrents drown.
> *(8:5-7)*

S. Quinizio tells of how he is deeply moved by the statement "love is strong as death", because it means that now those who weep can be happy, and so also can those who are dead because they receive new life *(Speranza, p.173)*. In verse 5, the companions, the daughters of Jerusalem, introduce the couple, by echoing the question we heard earlier in the book *(see 3:6)*. The Good News Bible translation "arm in arm with her lover" conveys the sense of the Hebrew.

"I awakened you under the apple tree". This is the time of the new birth, like the songs of joy of Saint Francis. It is the time of the new birth of love and the new spring.

In *8:6* where we hear of the seal on the heart, the bride wishes to express the total giving of herself by a seal. A seal of metal was used to authenticate documents *(Ex 28:12)*. Also the seal could be carried by the owner on the finger *(Gn 41:42; Jr 22:24)* or on the arm as an armband. The seal can be worn on a pendant or a little chain *(Gn 38:18, Pr 3:3)*. The bride is one with the bridegroom – they are "one flesh".

This union can now never be destroyed even by death. Sheol in the Bible is the place of the living dead, but love overcomes this. The Canticle in this poetic form anticipates the victory of Jesus over death by love, and his offer of new life to all of us. Love overcomes death and is eternal.

The flames of love cannot be extinguished. The flames of love are divine flames, literally "flames of Yahweh". It is like the flame that burnt but did not consume Mount Horeb *(Ex 3:2)*. It is the living flame of love; that is the Spirit; that burns in the hearts of God's holy ones.

All love participates in its own unique way in the Love of God. It is this love that vivifies and gives life. It is Dante's love that moves the sun and the stars.

The great waters of verse 7 are like the "great waters" that are mentioned in the Old Testament. These waters are an image of chaos, of nothingness. In *Ps 69* we hear the psalmist say:

> Save me God! The water
> > is already up to my neck!
> I am sinking in the deepest swamp,
> > there is no foothold;
> I have stepped into deep water
> > and the waves are washing over me.
>
> Worn out with calling, my throat is hoarse,
> my eyes are strained, looking for my God.
> > *(Ps 69:1-4)*

Yet no floods can quench this love – no hatred, no power can take away love's victory. In St. Paul's letter to the Romans we read of the "love of God poured into our hearts by the Spirit given us" *(5:6)*. The love of God has come to us through Jesus. In chapter 8 we read Paul's hymn to God's love:

> After saying this, what can we add? With God on our side who can be against us? Since God did not spare his own Son, but gave him up to benefit us all, we may be certain, after such a gift, that he will not refuse anything he can give. Could anyone accuse those that God has chosen? When God acquits, could anyone condemn? Could Christ Jesus? No! He not only died for us – he rose from the dead, and there at God's right hand he stands and pleads for us.
> Nothing therefore can come between us and the love of Christ, even if we are troubled or worried, or being persecuted, or lacking food or clothes, or being threatened or even attacked. As scripture promised: *For your sake we are being massacred daily, and reckoned as sheep for the slaughter*. These are the trials through which we triumph, by the power of him who loved us.

> For I am certain of this: neither death nor life, no angel, no prince, nothing that exists, nothing still to come, not any power, or height or depth, nor any created thing, can ever come between us and the love of God made visible in Christ Jesus our Lord.
> *(Rom 8:31-39)*

Fyodor Dostoevsky, Modern Apostle of Compassionate Love:

Dorothy Day (1897-1980) when she worked with the poor in New York was very fond of quoting the monk Zossima in Dostoevsky's *The Brothers Karamazov*. There he says:

> ... love in action is a harsh and dreadful thing compared with love in dreams. Love in dreams is greedy for immediate action, rapidly performed and in the sight of all. Men will even give their lives if only the ordeal does not last long but is soon over, with all looking on and applauding as though on the stage. But active love is labour and fortitude, and for some people too perhaps a complete science. But I predict that just when you see with horror that in spite of all your efforts you are getting further from your goal, instead of nearer to it – at that very moment I predict that you will reach it and behold clearly the miraculous power of the Lord who has been all the time loving and mysteriously guiding you.

The Brothers Karamazov was Dostoevsky's masterpiece and was written towards the end of his life. He was at the height of his powers and spoke at the unveiling of a monument to Pushkin in 1880. But the novelist was himself by this time reaching the end of his own life. He was to be dead only six months later. The weight of all the suffering he had endured, the humiliation inflicted upon him in the late 1840s by Turgenev among others, the mock execution by firing squad to which he was subjected by Tsar Nicholas I, the years in the Siberian prison camp, the years of desperate grasping for a woman's love, his addiction to gambling (which he conquered), his life-long financial difficulties, to say nothing of his constant bouts of epilepsy and his worsening emphysema, all of these trials and tribulations had almost exhausted his body by the time he stepped onto the platform in front of a vast crowd at the Nobles Club on the evening of 8th June. He looked tired and grey, his body shrunken inside his dress coat.

Yet throughout the whole of his stormy life Dostoevsky had known himself to be 'a ball of fire', the flame of the spirit. When imprisoned in the Peter and Paul fortress, for instance, he had written, 'I have such a reserve of vitality that it cannot be exhausted.' And from the prison camp at Omsk he had told his brother that he retained 'healthy reserves of spiritual life'. While in the depths of his most trying years he was delighted to report that he had 'the vitality of a cat'. These words proved to be no idle boast when the grey, shrunken figure on the platform of the Nobles Club was transformed once more into a ball of fire as his words drew ever more thunderous applause from his audience. At the end of his speech they acclaimed him with cries such as 'You are our saint! You are our prophet!' and for a whole half-hour they recalled him back to the platform over and over again.

Children and Childhood:

Children were very precious to Fydor: We hear a note of passionate concern that children should be treasured and accorded dignity and compassion at all times. That note did not arise out of remote, sentimental theorizing but out of his own experience, not only in the forbidding back streets of St. Petersburg but also from the many visits he made to homes for orphan children and illegitimate children, as well as to settlements for juvenile delinquents. His never-failing compassion for these unfortunates must often have startled the educated classes who read his Diary – as, for instance, when he proposed that since foundling children had been given such a raw deal from birth it was incumbent upon society to make up for their misfortune by ensuring that they were given privileged access to university education and afterwards helped to find a stable position in society. Nor within the whole 'theology of faces' permeating *The Brothers Karamazov* is any more powerful than the one expressed by Father Zossima when he says, 'Every day and every hour, every minute examine yourself and watch over yourself to make sure that your appearance is seemly. You pass by a little child, you pass spitefully with foul language and a wrathful heart; you may not have noticed the child, but he has seen you, and your face, ugly and profane, will perhaps remain in his defenceless heart. You may not know it, but you have perhaps sown an evil seed in him and it may grow.'

(Nicholl, Triumphs of the Spirit, p.171)

Dostoevsky's own childhood was happy. He would remark that from his earliest childhood he was able to look with joy at the love he received. His earliest memory came from when he was three years old. The governess had just brought him into the room and asked him to say the evening prayer in the presence of house guests. Fyodor knelt before the icon and recited his prayer: "Dear Mother of God, all my hope is in thee – give me shelter under thy wing." Dostoesky never forgot this prayer. He repeated it all his life and taught it to his children. "I came from a pious Russian family," he said as an adult. "In our family we knew the Gospels almost from the cradle". However, his soul was extraordinarily sensitive and did not have the protection and defence mechanisms that others use to shield them from reality. For instance, some religious people use pious platitudes to shield them in the face of unspeakable tragedy.

When Dostoevsky was a young child he had an experience that was to stay with him for the rest of his life. In Joseph Franks' biography of Dostoevsky he gives an account of an exchange between Dostoevsky and a close friend, Sofya:

> Dostoevsky spoke quickly, agitatedly and stumblingly ... The most frightful, the most terrible sin – was to violate a child. To take a life – that is horrible, Dostoevsky said, but to take away faith in the beauty of love – that is the most terrible crime. And Dostoevsky recounted an episode from his childhood. When I lived in Moscow as a child in a hospital for the poor, Dostoevsky said, where my father was a doctor, I played with a little girl (the daughter of a coachman or a cook). She was a delicate, graceful child of nine ... And some disgraceful wretch violated the girl when drunk and she died, pouring out blood. I recall, Dostoevsky said, being sent for my father in the other wing of the hospital, but it was too late. All

> my life this memory has haunted me as the most frightful crime, the most terrible sin, for which there is not, and cannot be, any forgiveness, and I punished Stavrogin in The Devils with this very same terrible crime.
> *(Dostoevsky, The Miraculous Years, p.21)*

Dostoevsky saw how precious the child was in himself or herself. He measured compassion by the way we treat the vulnerable, especially the most vulnerable of all God's creatures. The broken body of his little friend showed the broken spirit. Those who kill the body are murderers – those who rape and abuse the vulnerable are soul murderers. This was an impassioned theme in his writing. In this he echoed and made real for us Jesus' teaching about welcoming the little ones and not turning them away. Anyone who welcomes a little child welcomes Jesus *(see Mt 18:5)*. There is another article he wrote in his journal *A Writers Diary*. He did not deny the validity of science but he argued a more critical spirit to the way the insights of science are used. He echoed Péguy here who urged a critical spirit to science and its findings and uses. When numbers, -isms, replace the dignity of people then we become brutalized. He wrote the following:

> If science is unable to provide for people's subsistence, and there is a shortage of space, people are going to throw their babies into latrines, or eat them. I won't be surprised if they do both, especially if science suggests it to them ... When food becomes scarce and science proves unable to provide for food and fuel, whereas the world population continues to rise, it will be necessary to stop the further growth of population. Science says it isn't your fault nature has arranged things that way, and the instinct of self-preservation being first and foremost, it follows that babies must be burnt. That is the morality of science. The burning of babies will become habitual, for all moral principles in man are only relative if he has to rely on nothing but his own strength ... Science by itself, as it reaches the point when it becomes insensitive to the death of babies, will deaden and brutalize mankind. But with Christianity even the shortage of food

and fuel could be overcome – one can always choose to die oneself, for the sake of one's brother, rather than kill off babies.

Jesus' touchstone was the treatment of children. The disciples tried to block them from coming to him but he welcomed them and blessed them *(see Mk 9:33-37, 10:13-16 et passim)*. He also spoke severely against those who would become a scandal and hurt one of the little ones *(see Mt 18:5-7)*. Yet it was the spirit of childhood that was to lead to the writer discovering Christ again. When he was a political prisoner in Siberia he was tempted to despair and to give up. He met a young man named Ali, a Muslim, who was wrongly imprisoned. Ali read the New Testament with Fydor. All around them was cruelty and horror that for a time threatened to destroy Fydor, but his constant reading of the New Testament with his Muslim friend who loved Jesus was a preparation.

In his *Diary of a Writer* for February 1876 he tells us how on Easter Day 1852, when he was serving as a political prisoner in Siberia, he was so disgusted by the drunkenness and violence of his fellow-prisoners that he climbed on to his bunk and turned his back upon the hell of a barrack room. For a long time he nursed his loathing of the other prisoners until there suddenly arose within him the memory of an incident which he had completely forgotten from twenty years past.

As a child of nine he had one day been wandering alone across an open field on their estate when he thought he heard a wolf approaching. In his terror he ran towards the lonely figure of Marei, the serf who was ploughing the field. Marei quickly comforted the boy, stroking him on the cheek and murmuring, 'Don't be frightened, my dear. Christ be with thee. Cross thyself.'

'But I did not cross myself', writes Dostoevsky, 'the corners of my mouth quivered; and, I believe, that was what impressed him most. Slowly he stretched out his thick thumb, with the black nail soiled with earth, and gently touched my trembling lips ... and he looked at me with a long motherly smile.' And now, twenty years later, it was Marei's soil-blackened thumb that Dostoevsky particularly remembered:

and if I had been his own son he could not have bestowed upon me a glance full of a more serene love. And yet, who had prompted him? He was a peasant serf, while I was a nobleman's son. No one would find out how he had caressed me and no one would reward him. The meeting was a solitary one, in an open field; and only God, maybe, perceived from above what a profound and enlightened human feeling, what delicate, almost womanly tenderness may fill the heart of some ignorant Russian peasant serf. And when I climbed down off my bunk and gazed around I felt I could behold these unfortunate men with a wholly different outlook, for suddenly, by some miracle, all the hatred and anger had completely vanished from my heart.

That is a classic illustration of the melting of the heart which is essential if one is to see one's fellow human beings in the light of the Holy Spirit. And the fact that Russians have a special word for such a moment – *umilenie* – is itself testimony to the frequency with which they have been alert to those moments throughout the long history of the Russian people's spiritual endeavour. That moment of *umilenie* in 1852 gave an impulse to the spirit of Dostoevsky that was to sustain him for the rest of his life throughout many trials and failures. For he was aware, first, that, however inchoately, he had found his way into the heart of the Russian people. Secondly, he had rediscovered Christ, and more specifically 'the Russian Christ'; and thereby he saw opening up before him, more clearly than ever, the trajectory of his vocation as a writer.

(see Triumphs of the Spirit in Russia, p.160f)

The Russian Jesus that Dostoevsky spoke of did not mean that Jesus belonged to Russia alone. He did mean, however, that the Russians always had a special affinity with the crucified and forsaken Christ who was one with them in their struggles.

The Christ of Dostoevsky:

Anna Grigorievna Dostoevska wrote in her reminiscences of when she and her husband looked at a picture of Holbein the Younger's *Dead Christ*. She said:

> The painting had a crushing impact on Fyodor Mikhailovich. He stood there as if stunned. And I did not have the strength to look at it – it was so painful for me, particularly in my sickly condition – and I went into other rooms. When I came back after fifteen or twenty minutes, I found him still riveted to the same spot in front of the painting. His agitated face had a kind of dread in it, something I had noticed more than once during the first moments of an epileptic seizure.
>
> Quietly I took my husband by the arm, led him to another room and sat him down on a bench, expecting the attack from one minute to the next. Luckily this did not happen. He calmed down little by little and left the museum, but insisted on returning once again to view this painting which had struck him so powerfully.

That was the first time Dostoevsky realized in the depth of his being the reality of the sufferings of Jesus. He would use the experience to good effect in *The Idiot*. For Dostoevsky the decisive message of Jesus is the message of love. This is the essence of religion for him. Love is expressed in compassion. Dostoevsky could help the readers see this.

One of the most moving instances of how Dostoevsky drew his readers into his own experience and helped them to ease their own sufferings is contained in the chapter of *The Brothers Karamazov* entitled 'Women of faith'. There Father Zossima asks a woman weeping over the death of her three-year-old boy where she comes from. 'From far away, far away', she said in a sing-song voice. In response Father Zossima gently speaks to her in such a way as to draw the bitterness out of her heart. And then he asks the woman what was the child's name. 'Alexei, dear father.' 'A lovely name! After Alexsei, the man of God?' says Zossima. 'Of God, dear father; of God.'

Alexsei was actually the name of Dostoevsky's three-year-old child who had himself died only a few months previously. And doubtless Father Zossima's words were akin to those spoken by the *starets* Ambrose of the Optino hermitage to Dostoevsky himself when he went there in June 1878 accompanied by his young friend, the philosopher Vladimir Solovyov. And we are privileged to catch a glimpse of a singular thread linking the peasant woman to the writer, to the *starets* and the court of the Tsar when we learn of Dostoevsky, in April 1880, reading the chapter 'Women of faith' to a gathering of a court circle. Among them was Princess Marya Feodorovna, the wife of the future Tsar Alexander III. She had herself not long before lost a little son. She was moved to tears by Dostoevsky's reading and grateful for the balm he brought.

More than all the other evangelists, St. John sees the miracle in a Christ who proclaims love to an evil world. Dostoevsky emphasized the following passages from St. John:

> A new commandment I give unto you. That ye love one another; as I have loved you, that ye also love one another. *(John 13:34)*

> This is my commandment, That ye love one another, as I have loved you.
> *(John 15:12)*

> He that loveth his brother abideth in the light, and there is no occasion of stumbling in him. *(I John 2:10)*

> Beloved, let us love one another: for love is of God; and every one that loveth is born of God, and knoweth God. *(I John 4:7)*

> No man hath seen God at any time. If we love one another, God dwelleth in us, and his love is perfected in us. *(I John 4:12)*

> We love him, because he first loved us.
> If a man say, I love God, and hateth his brother, he is

a liar: for he that loveth not his brother whom he hath seen, how can he love God whom he hath not seen?

And this commandment have we from him, That he who loveth God love his brother also. *(I John 4:19-21)*

Dostoevsky tried to paint a Christ figure in Prince Myshkin in *The Idiot* but he was too angelic; his public had to await the more human figures of Zossima and Alyosha in *The Brothers Karamazov*. Compassion was the whole of Christianity for Dostoevsky.

Dante in his *Inferno* explored through the different characters mindsets of sin that lead us from God. It wouldn't be fair to call the *Inferno* a confession yet Dante analyzed the states of mind that lead us astray. Dostoevsky explores the demons that beset the modern mind and lead us from true compassion. He provides a therapy in this in that he unmasks our securities. In his work *The Idiot* it is true that the Prince is unable to change the world, but what would a world be without a world full of princes like Myshkin. An ideal may be unattainable, but to strive after anything else is not worth the world.

Yet the idiot prince is a success in his own way because for a moment he is able to kindle the faith in others of a truer image of themselves. Myshkin's aim is to bring people to a new state of being:

> This "state of being" is one of communion and unity with the all, with God, and hence with nature and humanity. Somewhat surprisingly the explicit statement to this effect is made by Ippolit and not by Prince Myshkin: "In scattering the seed, scattering your 'charity,' your kind deeds, you are giving away, in one form or another, part of your personality, and taking into yourself part of another; you are in mutual communion with one another … All your thoughts, all the seeds scattered by you, perhaps forgotten by you, will grow up and take form" (Terras, *The Idiot: An Interpretation*, p.79).

Dostoevsky was very struck by the Johannine image of the Word made flesh. The Word is a light in the darkness, a light that cannot be overcome *(Jn 1:1-18)*. In the darkness of the world Dostoevsky shows the light in a new way and like Prince Myshkin he sows seeds that will give birth to new life. He helps prepare for the New Jerusalem clothed in the good works of good people.

Nicholas Berdyaev writes of Dostoevsky's contribution in the following inspired passage:

> The work of Dostoevsky is the climax of Russian literature and it is the finest expression of its earnest, religious, tormented character; its path of sorrow led to Dostoievsky, and all the shadows of Russian life and history were gathered together in him. But there was a glimmer of light, shining through a crack in the old world. The tragedy of Dostoevsky, like all true tragedy, involves purification and release, though those who are held by it in unescapable darkness, who accept only its misery, do not understand this. There is freeing of the spirit and joy to be had from reading Dostoevsky, the joy that one gets from suffering. It is the path the Christian has to tread. Dostoevsky renewed faith in man and in the notion of his depths, which Humanism had not recognized. Humanism destroys man, but he is born again if he believes in God – and only on this condition can he believe in himself. Dostoevsky does not dissociate faith in man from faith in Christ, the God-man. Throughout his life he had kept a skeptical reverence, a sort of mystical love, for that divine face, and it was in Christ's name and for love of him that he gave up that humanitarian circle whose prophet was Bielinsky. This faith of his Dostoevsky tested in the crucible of his doubts and tempered with their fire. He wrote in one of his notebooks: "No other expression of atheism has ever had such force in Europe [as humanitarianism]. It was not as a child that I learnt to believe in Christ and confess his faith. My Hosanna has burst forth from a

huge furnace of doubt." He had then lost his youthful belief in Schillerism, by which name he designated the cult of the "great and beautiful" – idealistic humanitarianism. In his experience Schillerism had not survived a single test, while his faith in Christ had stood up to them all; so he gave up the humanitarian belief in man and believed in him in the Christian way, deepening and strengthening that faith. For that very reason Dostoevsky could not be a pessimistic and despairing writer; there is always light in his darkness, and it is the light of Christ. It is indeed true that he shows man wandering among the chasms of inner division (it is a fundamental theme in his work), but this division does not in the end destroy the identity of the individual person. The image of man is restored through the God-man.
(Dostoevsky, p31f)

In the end love is strong as death and no evil or darkness can win in the end. Dostoevsky offers hope in a redeemed humanity in Christ even in the midst of a world that offers all darkness.

> Love no floods can quench,
> no torrents drown.
> *(Sg 8:7)*

Final Word: The Wedding Feast at Cana:

The wedding feast at Cana was where Jesus began his mission. It is told in the Gospel of John, chapter 2:1-12. John's account of the wedding goes as follows:

> On the third day there was a wedding at Cana in Galilee. The mother of Jesus was there, and Jesus and his disciples had also been invited. And they ran out of wine, since the wine provided for the feast had all been used, and the mother of Jesus said to

him, "They have no wine." Jesus said, "Woman, what do you want from me? My hour has not come yet." His mother said to the servants, *"Do whatever he tells you"*. There were six stone water jars standing there, meant for the ablutions that are customary among the Jews: each could hold twenty or thirty gallons. Jesus said to the servants, "Fill the jars with water", and they filled them to the brim. Then he said to them, "Draw some out now and take it to the president of the feast". They did this; the president tasted the water, and it had turned into wine. Having no idea where it came from – though the servants who had drawn the water knew – the president of the feast called the bridegroom and said, "Everyone serves good wine first and the worse wine when the guests are well wined; but you have kept the best wine till now".

This was the first of Jesus' signs: it was at Cana in Galilee. He revealed his glory, and his disciples believed in him. After this he went down to Capernaum with his mother and his brothers and his disciples, but they stayed there only a few days.

John begins his account "on the third day". From the time Jesus met John the Baptist until Cana takes 7 days. The fourth day saw the call of Philip and Nathaniel (from Cana) (1:43-51). Now three days later comes the feast. Many exegetes see the 7 days as referring to the seven days of creation (Gn 1:1 – 2:3).

Aristide Serra suggests an alternative, often reading such Jewish texts as the Targum of the Pseudo Jonathan, which says that the third day corresponds to the giving of the law to Moses (Ex 19). At Cana, on the third day, Jesus gives the new wine of revelation so that his disciples come to believe in him.

Jesus asks Mary (in a literal translation) "what is that to me and to you, woman". Often in John's gospel, Jesus speaks in parables in ways that people do not immediately understand (16:25, 29), passing from truly material considerations to the spiritual reality that lies behind the human reality. When Jesus speaks this way, his listeners do not understand. This method of rabbinic dialogue is seen with Jesus and his disciples in the episode with the Samaritan woman (4:31 – 34). In chapter 16:29, the disciples speak of Jesus using "veiled language". He shows his disciples in this way that he is led by the will of the Father. Many understand this and now tell the servants "do whatever he tells you" and the water becomes wine.

There is still another enigmatic term used by Jesus – he calls Mary, "woman". This is not a normal address for a son to his mother, so once again Jesus speaks in a symbolic role to show Mary's place in his community. Romanos the Melodist (d. ca. 560) wrote a hymn showing the link between Cana and Calvary. Romanos was born is Syria of a Jewish family, he converted to Christianity as a youth and went to what was then call Constantinople. In his poem "Mary, at the cross" he begins his reflection in the following way:

> Come, let us all celebrate him who was crucified for us: for Mary looked on him upon the cross and said: "Though you endure crucifixion, yet you are my son, my God".
> Worn out with grief, Mary, the ewe, seeing her own lamb taken to the slaughter, followed with the other women and cried: "Where are you going, my child? For whose sake are you finishing this swift race? Is there another marriage in Cana, and are you hastening there now to change the water into wine for them? Shall I go with you, child, or shall I rather wait for you? Speak to me, O Word; do not pass me by in silence: for you kept me in my purity, my son, my God.
> "I never thought that I would see you, my child, in such necessity nor did I ever believe that the lawless would rage so, and unjustly stretch out their hands against you: for still their infants cry "Hosanna" to you: still the road is strewn with palm-branches proclaiming to all how the lawless had sung your praises. And now a worse deed is done, and for whose sake? Alas; how is my light snuffed out, how to a cross is nailed my son, my God.
> "You are going to unjust slaughter, my child, and no one is suffering with you. Peter does not go with you. Peter who had said to you: "Never shall I deny you even though I die". Thomas deserted you, Thomas who cried. "Let us all die with him". The others too, the friends and companions who were to judge the tribes of Israel, where are they now? None of them is here: but one, alone, for the sake of them all, you are dying, my child;

because instead of them you have saved all, because instead of them you have loved all, my son, my God".

Jesus goes on in the hymn to speak to Mary assuring her that he willingly accepts death so that others may have life. She is to go "after the third day" of the resurrection and bring his comfort to others who cry out "where is God?", but for the time being she has to endure the pain of loss and loneliness as she stands at the cross.
John's account of the death of Jesus goes as follows:

> Near the cross of Jesus stood his mother and his mother's sister, Mary the wife of Clopas, and Mary of Magdala. Seeing his mother and the disciple he loved standing near her, Jesus said to his mother: "Woman, this is your son." Then to the disciple he said: "This is your mother". And from that hour the disciple made a place for her in his home.
> After this, Jesus knew that everything had now been completed, and to fulfill the scripture perfectly he said: *"I am thirsty"*.
> A jar-full of vinegar stood there, so putting a sponge soaked in the vinegar on a hyssop stick they held it up to his mouth. After Jesus had taken the vinegar he said, "it is accomplished"; and bowing his head he gave up his spirit.
> (Jn 19:25-30)

Here again the term "woman" is used. She is the woman of the new creation, the new covenant, the mother of the living. In Jesus death and resurrection Mary has a new role in helping giving birth to Christ in the hearts of those who will be like the "Beloved Disciple" who stood with her at the cross. When this new community is established, Jesus cries out after taking the vinegar "it is accomplished" (*tetelestai*). The Greek word means it has been accomplished. By dying he has overcome death and will rise again "on the third day." Now there is a new community of Mary and those who stood with her are the beloved disciples like the motley group of disciples of love whom I have meditated on in my life and whose vision I shared with you in these "word pictures". In v. 30 we read that "Jesus gave up his spirit". The Greek word is *paredoken* which means give out, hand over.

Mary and the beloved disciple now share in the life of the Spirit, the new wine. "On the third day", Jesus rose from the dead and this message is confirmed. This is the background to Cana and Mary's place. It is now interesting to turn to Dostoevsky and see how all these themes are part of his use of the feast of Cana in the "Brothers Karamazov".

The scene plays a central part in *The Brothers Karamazov*. Alyosha had suffered a great shock. The elder Zossima is dead and his body stank. *The Brothers Karamazov* became known as the book of smells. Those who were jealous were delirious with happiness. Dostoevsky parodies jealous clerics in the form of Fr. Ferrapont. Alyosha had just returned from Grushenka who had tried to seduce him. Marilyn Monroe is reputed to have wished to play Grushenka. Grushenka had been abused as a young girl but in Alyosha she meets only love. This is a moment of grace for her. Now Alyosha returns to the monastery and here begins his dream:

> *"And the third day there was a marriage in Cana of Galilee;"* read Father Paissy. *"And the mother of Jesus was there; and both Jesus was called, and his disciples, to the marriage."*
> "Marriage? What's that ... A marriage!" floated whirling through Alyosha's mind. "There is happiness for her, too ... She has gone to the feast ... No, she has not taken the knife ... That was only a tragic phrase ... Well ... tragic phrases should be forgiven, they must be. Tragic phrases comfort the heart ... without them, sorrow would be too heavy for men to bear. Rakitin has gone off to the back-alley. As long as Rakitin broods over his wrongs, he will always go off to the back-alley ... But the high road ... the road is wide and straight and bright as crystal, and the sun is at the end of it ... Oh, what' being read? ..."
> *"And when they wanted wine, the mother of Jesus saith unto him; 'They have no wine' ..."* Alyosha heard.
> "Ah, yes, I was missing that, and I didn't want to miss it, I love that passage; it's Cana of Galilee, the first

miracle ... Ah, that miracle! Ah, that sweet miracle! It was not men's grief but their joy Christ visited; He worked His first miracle to help men's gladness, too ... 'There's no living without joy,' Mitya says ... Yes, Mitya ... 'Everything that is true and good is always full of forgiveness,' he used to say that, too ..."

"*Jesus saith unto her, Woman, what has it to do with thee or me? Mine hour is not yet come.*

"*His mother saith unto the servants: Whatsoever he saith unto you, do it ...*"

"Do it ... Gladness, the gladness of some poor, very poor, people ... Of course they were poor, since they hadn't wine enough even at a wedding ... The historians write that in those days the people living about the Lake of Gennesaret were the poorest that can possibly be imagined ... and another great heart, that other great being, His mother, knew that He had come not only to make His great terrible sacrifice. She knew that His heart was open even to the simple, artless merrymaking of some obscure and unlearned people, who had warmly bidden Him to their poor wedding. 'Mine hour is not yet come,' He said, with a soft smile. (He must have smiled gently to her.) And indeed was it to make wine abundant at poor weddings He had come down to earth? And yet He went and did as she asked Him ... Ah, he is reading again ..."

"*Jesus saith unto them, Fill the waterpots with water. And they filled them up to the brim.*

"*And he saith unto them, Draw out now and bear unto the governor of the feast. And they did it.*

"*When the ruler of the feast had tasted the water that was made wine and knew not whence it was (but the servants which drew the water knew), the governor of the feast called the bridegroom,*

"*And saith unto him: Every man at the beginning doth set forth good wine; and when men have well drunk, that which is worse; but thou hast kept the good wine until now.*"

"But what's this, what's this? Why is the room growing wider? ... Ah, yes ... It's the marriage, the wedding ... yes, of course. Here are the guests, here is the young couple sitting, and the merry crowd and ... Where is the wise governor of the feast? But who is this? Who? Again the walls are receding ... Who is getting up there from the great table? What! ... He here, too? But he's in the coffin ... but he's here, too. He has stood up, he sees me, he is coming here ... Oh, God!"

Then Alyosha in his dream saw the dead Zossima come towards him. The elder speaks to Alyosha:

> The elder raised Alyosha by the hand, and he rose from his knees.
> "We are rejoicing," the little, thin old man went on. "We are drinking the new wine, the wine of new, great gladness; do you see how many guests? Here are the bride and bridegroom, here is the wise governor of the feast, he is tasting the new wine. Why do you wonder at me? I gave an onion to a beggar, so I too am here. And many here have given only an onion each – only one little onion ... What are all our deeds? And you, my gentle one, you, my kind boy, you too have known how to give a famished woman an onion today. Begin your work, dear one, begin it, gentle one! ... Do you see our Sun, do you see Him?"
> "I am afraid ... I dare not look," whispered Alyosha.
> "Do not fear Him. He is terrible in His greatness, awful in His sublimity, but infinitely merciful. He has made Himself like unto us from love and rejoices with us. He is changing the water into wine so that the gladness of the guests may not be cut short. He is expecting new guests; He is calling new ones unceasingly for ever and ever ... There they are bringing new wine. Do you see they are bringing the vessels ..."
> Something glowed in Alyosha's heart, something

filled it till it ached, tears of rapture rose from his soul ...
He stretched out his hands, uttered a cry and awoke.

Again the coffin, the open window, and the soft, solemn, distinct reading of the Gospel. But Alyosha did not listen to the reading.

Alyosha awakens and leaves the monastery. On his way he reflects:

Alyosha stood, gazed, and suddenly threw himself down on the earth. He did not know why he embraced it. He could not have told why he longed so irresistibly to kiss it, to kiss it all. But he kissed it weeping, sobbing, and watering it with his tears and vowed passionately to love it, to love it for ever and ever. "Water the earth with the tears of your joy and love those tears," echoed in his soul.

What was he weeping over?

Oh! in his rapture he was weeping even over those stars, which were shining at him from the abyss of space, and "he was not ashamed of that ecstasy." There seemed to be threads from all those innumerable worlds of God, linking his soul to them, and it was trembling all over "in contact with other worlds." He longed to forgive everyone for everything, and to beg forgiveness – oh not for himself but for all men, for all and for everything. "And others are praying for me, too," echoed again in his soul. But with every instant he felt clearly and, as it were, tangibly, that something firm and unshakable as that vault of heaven had entered into his soul. It was as though some idea has seized the sovereignty of his mind – and it was for all his life and for ever and ever. He had fallen on the earth a weak boy, but he rose up a resolute champion, and he knew and felt it suddenly at the very moment of his ecstasy. And never, never, all his life long, could Alyosha forget that minute.

"Someone visited my soul in that hour," he used to say afterwards, with implicit faith in his words.

Within three days he left the monastery in

accordance with the words of his elder, who had bidden him "sojourn in the world."

Alyosha learnt from Zossima that our happiness is God's concern. Zossima's commission to Alyosha was to go to the world and leave the monastery to lead people to live God's dream. At the end of the book Alyosha gathers a group of children around him who come to learn from Alyosha and find happiness in God. The children Alyosha gathers remember the sad and lonely death of Ilyusha. The final gathering of the children takes place at the stone where Ilyusha and his father used to feed the birds, but Ilyusha suffered from the cruelty of others, including the children and he dies a lonely death. Alyosha gathers the children and says "Let us make a contract, here at Ilyusha's stone, that we will never forget, first, Ilyushenhka and, secondly, one other." Alyosha, recalling Jesus with others, begins to found his little community of beloved disciples. The boys are all guilty. They have hurt Ilyusha but now they seek forgiveness and hope to begin a new life. This is Alyosha's way of changing water into wine. As the poet W.H. Auden said.

> "In the deserts of the heart
> let the healing fountain start".

Printed in Great Britain
by Amazon